RICHARD COBB:
PART TWO:
COBB 18-30

(Uni, jobs, a taxi & other obstacles).

Richard Cobb

*For everyone that was kind enough to read my first
book and helped me finish this one. Thank You.*

CONTENTS

Freshers Week:

Freshers Week was exactly as I had envisaged it. Lots of drinking, lots of over-exuberance, lots of kebabs, little sleep, and absolutely no attention whatsoever from anyone of the opposite sex (or from anyone of the same sex, basically I wasn't getting attention from anyone). There was an infamous club night called Shagtag which was every bit as bad as it sounds. It was essentially an interactive Tinder game. The drill was you'd pay £3 to go into a club which was so rammed that even the walls were sweating. After queuing for what felt like an eternity, you'd be given a sticker with a number on it. There was a wall where you could write a message for the owner of said number like, 'Hey number 114 meet me by the bins in 5, love from 87 xxx.' This all seemed like a thoroughly confusing set of instructions for people that weren't exactly in any fit state to follow a set of instructions which could have quite easily been lifted right out of a *Saw* film. I didn't carry out an exit poll, but I got the feeling that those of us that were perched anxiously by the wall for a message from our secret admirer was 2006's equivalent of those people that sit waiting in a desert with a machine gun strapped to the back of their 4x4 awaiting an alien invasion. Needless to say, the machine gun wasn't utilised that night. I can't write that can I? I'll swiftly move on and see if this makes it past the edit. After an hour or so sinking god-awful double vodka oranges, I went back to check my progress on the wall. I scanned the wall before having a quick glance at what my number was. It was only then it became clear that I'd not been issued with a number on entry in the first place, so the whole charade had essentially just been paying £3 to watch people get off with each other from the side-lines, like a young Attenborough quietly commentating on a herd of rabid wildebeest. The early signs were out that this wasn't the picture of university that *American Pie* had painted. Much like the first book, the unfortunate narrative was essentially the same as it had been in high school.

The following night I spent £20 on a pub crawl hoping my fortunes would change. Arriving at the first pub, I was issued with a nice baby blue t-shirt with 'FRESHERS 06' emblazoned across the chest and an optimistic list of pubs on the back. My friends and I wasted no time in throwing the t-shirts on to blend in with the rest of the certifiable bell-ends on the pub crawl. By pub two an early contender for first to be evicted from the group asked if he could sign our t-shirts. I immediately thought 'what a nice gesture. I mean it's a bit odd and self-absorbed to offer to sign something for somebody without them asking, but then again I signed a photo of me wearing a Hearts top at the age of ten which nobody asked for, so in a way this is every bit as reasonable.' I was up first; this would make for a nice reminder of the characters I met in my first year of university. There was no way this would go as badly as that unfortunate incident a few months previously when I left high school and my ex-girlfriend and her mates all happily signed my shirt only for her to break up with me three hours later before the ink had even dried. Luckily, the tears which would follow in generous portions smudged it, so that was comforting, but she could have at least written it in pencil. Anyway, back to our autograph happy new friend, he drew a cock and balls on the back of my shirt so I added that to the graveyard of signed shirts at the back of my cupboard which would never see the light of day again.

Freshers Week culminated in going to see a pop group called Infernal at the Potterow Student Union. Infernal had been a mediocre one-hit-wonder a year previously with their disgustingly catchy pop banger 'Paris to Berlin.' I hadn't kept tabs on them since, so I was going into this gig a bit blind, but sadly not deaf. The band swaggered out like Freddie Mercury at *Live Aid* to a 300 strong crowd of pissed-up punters who were all just looking for one thing. Unfortunately, Infernal mistook the one thing everyone in attendance was after to mean their song 'Paris to Berlin' so they decided to subject us all to it three times in a five-song set. It wasn't a good gig by any stretch, but luckily for Infernal, it was far from the worst performance of the year. They left that honour to me for my Building Surveying course which would commence three or four days later.

By the time I had been enrolled on the course, I'd long since missed the boat with student accommodation. As flats were few and far between, I crashed on a partially deflated lilo atop a couple of chairs in my friend's common room in Fountainbridge, around a fifteen-minute walk from the university for the first few weeks until I got a flat sorted.

It became glaringly obvious within a week or so that I had my work cut out if I was to stay afloat in this course. You know the faff involved when you're pouring milk on Weetabix, and the big greedy up-it-self Weetabix soaks up all the milk leaving none for the rest of the bowl to enjoy? Around 60% of the folk in my classes were big greedy (some of them up themselves) Weetabix that soaked up all the milk the lecturers could pour on them (this is a metaphor; it wasn't that sort of uni). In contrast, I was sat there like a Sainsbury's own Weetabix getting Chinese water tortured in milk for hours on end with absolutely none of it sinking in.

The lectures I managed to drag myself along to, I'd sit there consuming barely any of what was being said to me, as though I'd inadvertently stumbled into a German class. Instead of owning up to my mistake, I'd just sit there perfecting my best concentration face, whilst under the surface praying that I didn't make eye contact with the lecturer when it was question time. When we'd be handed out some course work, I'd panic and inevitably "compare answers" with my mates. This technique would act as little more than a tiny air pocket within a massive water tank which I was handling about as well as a handcuffed Houdini (again, metaphor, it wasn't that sort of uni).

Looking back, I'm not exactly sure what I thought the outcome was going to be here, it had gotten to the point where my confidence in my ability had eroded to the point where I didn't feel comfortable attending lectures. My Ferris Bueller homage wasn't inspired through laziness; it was purely because I didn't feel comfortable attending when I wasn't retaining any information. This was particularly the case when there was a group project due as the only thing I had confidence in at that time was that I'd muck it up.

By that point, I'd moved into my first flat away from home with a friend from West Linton who was on the same course, which again was located around the Fountainbridge area of the city. It was a ground floor, one-bedroom flat which had been un-seamlessly turned into a microscopic two-bedroom flat at the expense of the living room.

There was no escaping that the flat was tiny, and nobody would argue with it being labelled a complete shithole. The Liam Gallagher poster acting as a curtain in the bathroom did little to douse the flames of acceptance, but it did the job, and that was all that mattered.

Bebo:

Long before Facebook reared its massive shiny over-moisturised forehead, Bebo was the platform to keep tabs on how wonderfully everyone else was getting on at university as they shared endless photos of glow stick parties, toga parties, no themed-parties, basically just parties. It was also an opportunity to catch up with the heathens that had taken a "gap yah" and went to work a "gruelling" three hour week in a beach bar in Thailand or hang out with an African tribe that looked absolutely raging at their unwarranted invasion.

Preceding Bebo, MSN Messenger was as close as you'd get to chatting to friends outwith face to face, texting or phoning. MSN taught harsh lessons in love and carried its own brutal brand of heartbreak when my heart would jump out of my chest as I saw the love of my life (that week) had logged in and then immediately logged back out again. Part of the ingredients of any teenager was being filled to the brim with vast quantities of self-pity. This meant the immediate presumption for the motive behind their swift logging off was that they had a quick scan down their contacts list, clocked I was on and thought 'fuck this' then immediately unplugged both their computer and dial-up internet at the wall to eliminate them from the risk of joining a conversation which, much like their computer, would lack any signs of electricity. Worse than that was the slow-burn of "brb" which stood for "be right back." The assumption, of course, being that they'd be "right back". The reality, they had absolutely no intention of being right back. I'd invest hours talking about bands I hated (at one remarkably low point I even conversed with someone about The Feeling...) just to try and jump-start some form of two-way conversation with a girl. When the inevitable right hook of "brb" landed, it was just a matter of time before they dropped off the conversation and I had to give myself a stern post-match talking down after another embarrassing performance.

Bebo, on the other hand, wasn't as unforgiving, but it was very political, or at least I treated it very politically. There was an option to "share the luv" which wasn't so much about sharing "luv" it was about trying desperately to get someone to notice you. To begin with, you were entrusted with one "luv" per day to use wisely, which I can only assume led to one too many domestics, so they upped their figure to three. You could share up to three hearts per day, and it was up to you to divide them up and hand them out as you pleased with seemingly no ground rules. Somewhat surprisingly, sharing three hearts with three different people didn't automatically swing open the magic doors to four-way gangbangs. Still, it seemed like a foolproof way of casually testing the water with someone that you fancied by firing a love arrow their way. If disaster struck and you were immediately landed with a "WTF?!" to your heart delivery there was always the watertight get-out clause of blaming it on an unidentified uni mate that had jumped on your computer when you weren't looking.

Similarly, the hugely stressful top 16 list brought its own baggage. The top 16 list would be visible on everyone's profile like a trophy cabinet. The etiquette was simple- if a friend or love interest promoted you to their coveted top 16, it was only polite to give them a mid to low table trial on your top 16 to reciprocate the goodwill gesture and to heighten the chance of staying on their list. If you slowly crept up the charts, it was a sign of success and meant shit was about to get real. If on the other hand, they relegated you from their friendship charts, it was fair game to boot their friendship into oblivion and never promote the bastard again. Finding out you'd dropped out of someone's top 16 during a routine stalk of their profile was as humiliating as it was devastating. So many questions and no reasonable way to approach such a ridiculous grievance. More often than not, it was probably just a simple spring cleaning or tactical squad rotation, but the tsunami of outrage it caused was beyond belief.

There was a way of attempting to bump up your credibility by answering polls on your page in the hope that someone would stumble upon it and suddenly fall madly in love with you. Once or twice I'd highball the "how many girls have you kissed" question on a poll or I'd go one further and say something like "Ooft, good bloody question! Lol, is there a character limit on this thing? How long have you got? Jeez, where to even begin. Brb. Do you mean this week or overall? I mean I couldn't even begin to hazard a guess in the fear that I'd break the hearts of every lucky recipient if I forgot the exact number." That was code for "Two."

The final and perhaps most significant deal on the emotional guillotine of Bebo was the option of choosing an "other half." The concept was straightforward, if you were coupled up with someone, you would likely be each other's other half, but if you weren't, it was an almighty bloodbath. It was a popular tactic to seek out a faux other half to provide a comfort blanket and to make any onlookers jealous. Comforting as this was, it wasn't without perils. You could be happily other halved with a close friend one day, then log on the next to see you were all alone and they'd moved on to pastures new without even having left a note in what felt like a modern-day equivalent of the night of the long knives. On the rare occasion over the years that I'd need to honourably resign from my post of being a loyal other half to someone, I'd feel intense guilt and worry that I was ruining their happiness. I was keen to know they had another eligible heir to their other half throne waiting in the wings that they could deploy as a back-up until they found someone to fill the void.

To summarise, Bebo and its predecessor MSN Messenger slowly but surely turned everyone into paranoid perverts and egomaniacs.

First Love/s Pt III:

Reconnecting with old friends who were no longer geographically close was the one real plus point of the early days of social media. A girl who I'd last seen back in **primary four** and you might recall from Part One after I'd lovingly drawn a picture of her which resembled Miss Piggy appeared on my Bebo one day as a friend of a friend. I felt my eyes well a little and my throat close up as I saw her. She looked amazing in her black and white profile picture. My hand was nervously trembling as I hovered over the add friend button and paused. I decided against adding her. It had been too long, and reaching out now completely out of the blue would be weird and creepy. The whole next day I couldn't stop thinking about her and I wondered how she was getting on. Returning to the uni computer lab later that night to carry out my weekly routine of watching the pop-culture phenomenon *The OC,* I saw how one of the main characters seemed to have incredible luck with the ladies just by showing a bit of confidence, sarcasm and self-belief in himself.

Feeling inspired I dug deep, and with my new-found superpowers of confidence and little shame I added her later that night along with a quick message 'Hey, I doubt you'll remember me, but I'm pretty sure we used to go to West Linton Primary School together.' I kept it short and low key as I wasn't overly convinced that she filed Miss Piggy-gate in the executive lounge of her memory like I had. The overarching feeling in the immediate aftermath of adding someone you harboured strong feelings for between the ages of five and eight was 'Oh dear. Oh, fucking hell! Unsend! Unsend!' It was too late; the deed was done. My brain wasn't fooling anyone with its hollow follow-up of 'Oh well, if worst comes to worst you can always just blame the message on a uni mate?' which would definitely not hold water in this scenario.

The following day the unthinkable happened (unless you saw this event unfolding, in which case the thinkable happened). She accepted my friend request. Her response was along the lines of 'Of course I remember you! I see you're living in Edinburgh? I've just moved back here to go to Edinburgh Uni. We should grab a coffee sometime soon.' Sceptics among you may question the likelihood of her asking me for a coffee and, to be fair, I'm slightly doubting the accuracy of my memory here. Then again, given how much of an internal struggle I had adding her as a friend, I sincerely doubt it was me that approached the suggestion of said coffee grabbing. We exchanged numbers and set a date for the big reunion.

Up until then, I hadn't bought into the idea of fate, but this had all the credentials for a modern tale as old as time. When I was seven, I submitted planning permission to my parents for 15 Fergusson View. The plan was simple, once my sister Julie moved out in five/six years to attend university they should let me knock down the adjoining wall between our bedrooms to form one big room so I could ask the girl at school to move in when we'd both grown up. My *Grand Designs* dream crumbled when she moved overseas the following year, and we moved out of the house four years later.

Did this Starbucks visit reignite the flame and lead us to eternal happiness? Did we buy the house in West Linton and knock down the wall to form the bedroom of dreams? No. I slept through my alarm, and I texted her in a panic to apologise for my no-show. No sooner had I clicked send when a message came through from her apologising that she had to go to the library as she had some uni work to do so we should reschedule. Several more failed coffee attempts ensued as we struggled to set a date that would suit, then eventually we just gave up.

It wasn't until six years later when I was in a club in Edinburgh's George Street that I passed her in the corridor. We kept walking in opposite directions like they do in that alternative ending of *The Butterfly Effect* (bloody hell that's a niche reference). I was in a relationship at the time, so I wasn't going to try any of my funny business, but I wouldn't be able to forgive myself if I didn't introduce myself to her face to face after all these years. I turned around and caught up with her just before she went out the door. The rest, as they say, is history. Forgotten history to be exact as I was hammered that night and woke up the next day without a single recollection of any of our brief conversation and we never crossed paths again. If I were to hazard a guess, I'd say her last words were "brb."

Late Goth Phase:

It's no secret that some humans mature quicker than others. Some could have full beards, a child or a mortgage by the age of eighteen; other unnamed individuals could have been trying throughout their twenties to desperately shepherd some hair onto their cheeks to no avail in a windowless broom cupboard on Leith Walk.

Goths were an ever-present shadowy figure between second and fourth year of high school, but then sort of flew off like bats by fifth and sixth year. I remember one guy in school who was still very much in the L plates phase of his goth career had written 'I love Satin' on his bag in permanent marker. Nobody had the heart to correct him, so his public affection for fine fabric remained on his bag alongside a Slipknot badge for the rest of the year.

Contrary to my dad's occasional light-hearted jibes because I had the one Marilyn Manson song everybody liked on my iPod, I was never a goth in high school. I wore black a lot, but when your school uniform consisted of black trousers, a black jumper, black shoes, and black socks, you were up against it to prove otherwise. I wasn't really invested in fashion or hanging about with crows in graveyards enough to conform to one social group, so I basically just dressed in whatever I felt comfortable in with no real affiliation to a particular colour.

When I was eighteen and at university, I was listening to bands like My Chemical Romance, Fall Out Boy, Placebo and The Horrors, many of whom had members with immaculate jet black hair which in the hallowed pages of NME and Q looked the business. Now I was living away from home, it felt like the perfect opportunity to experiment with my style a bit to see what happened. Without much thought or deliberation, I bought some black hair dye from Boots and hot-footed it back to the flat to begin the process of transforming myself into a moody music magazine cover star. I went all-in with the permanent stuff too, wash in wash out seemed like a pointless venture. As far as I was concerned, it was permanent or nothing. The instructions on the box seemed a bit excessive, so I read the first few lines and felt I had a good enough grasp to be able to ignore the rest of their advice. It was apparent incredibly early into proceedings that not reading the instructions fully was a fucking terrible decision. My scalp looked like a goth's ice cream on a warm day with dye rapidly abseiling down to my neck from all angles. Trying to stop it was a futile task, so I did what I could and then reverted to the now caked in black instructions to finish my self-administered makeover. Washing the dye over the shower, I wrote off a towel and then inspected the damage in the bathroom mirror. There were still clear streaks of black cascading down my forehead and diagonally across my neck. The first glance wasn't promising. I didn't look like any of my idols from the music magazines. Instead, I resembled a sad duck covered in oil from an RSPCA advert. I tried to wash them off again with no luck then messaged one of my friends to ask for some posthumous hair dyeing advice. 'You applied Vaseline to stop the dye from running, didn't you?' she wrote. By the tone of her text, I could deduce that it would have been a pretty sizeable mistake not applying Vaseline before dyeing my hair/bit of my face black so of course, that would be the one thing that I had forgotten to do. Several rewashes, mild panic attacks and heavy scrubs later the marks were mostly away, and I was left with what was rather underwhelmingly just a darker version of my hair. This would seem the obvious and desired outcome from dyeing your hair, but it wasn't nearly as groundbreaking as I had imagined it would be.

I went to see The Horrors in Glasgow a few weeks later as part of the annual NME tour with three other bands. Dundee band The View were the big draw on that night, so I wanted to make it abundantly clear that whilst I quite liked The View, I was predominantly there to see The Horrors who were probably best described as being a Goth rock/post-punk band back then. The band would be typically all dressed in black with drainpipe skinny jeans and big hair. I had neither skinny jeans nor big hair, so I thought I'd wear a black shirt and some black nail polish to nail my colours to the mast. Applying the nail polish to my left hand was surprisingly easy, given it was my first attempt at such a procedure. Things came unstuck when I tried to paint my right hand with my less accurate left hand. I gave up after a few failed landings so left the flat with just 50% of my fingernails dressed in black. To my disgruntlement, when I arrived at the venue, nobody seemed to bat an eyelid at me decked out in almost full goth home strip. The attention and feather-ruffling I'd been attempting with my new-found persona didn't really have the desired effect. If anything I was lowballing it given some of the efforts the band's fans had gone to that night with their back-combed hair, thick layer of eye-shadow and polka dot waistcoats. I left the gig early and got the train back to Edinburgh to go to the cinema with a few friends. I might not have been the biggest goth at the gig that night, but I was unquestionably the biggest goth at the 22:45 screening of *Rocky Balboa*.

That was the peak of my late goth phase, and I'd revert back to my usual jeans, hoody and obscure band t-shirt style shortly afterwards. It turned out dyeing my hair and painting my nails black didn't transform me into a photogenic goth-rock star in the same way that buying a trilby didn't make me Pete Doherty in his infamous constantly off his tits era. "Emo" was probably the more prevalent term for my darkened appearance and music taste at the time, but as I get older, I find myself mirroring my dad's outlook on subgenre intricacies, so I'm just going to blanket it as a goth phase.

New Beginnings, Different Ways:

Moments after my inevitable but nonetheless epic nosedive out of university in Edinburgh after less than a year, I moved back to my parents' house in the Scottish Borders with my tail firmly between my legs. Although this wasn't a big deal and financially it was a massive weight off, I felt like I was back at square one with little to show for my last year other than a seriously haemorrhaged bank account and a year-long hangover.

My parents were justifiably keen for me not to sit on my arse all day, so would use every opportunity to talk me up to potential employers. I wasn't even safe during a haircut. My mum would pick me up from the barbers and not so subtly enquire if the barber was interested in a unique opportunity to hire someone with zero experience of cutting hair and an apparent deficiency in eye contact and small talk. I'd turn up to car garages with a CV crumpled under my arm and a baggy suit, telling them how great I was with absolutely no evidence to reflect that on my CV like one of those smarmy eyeball grating frauds on *The Apprentice*. "Sure, I believe I could easily hit those sales figures. If anything, I think those targets are too low." I turned up to a job interview with an insurance company in Edinburgh and swaggered in as though I was the head of the company. First hurdle and I went head-first into the bushes "I suppose I think I'd be a good fit because my uncle works in insurance, so the knowledge runs in the family." "Oh, so what does your uncle do in insurance?" they naturally responded, to which I coolly replied "... Eh, well he does the eh usual sort of um insurance-y sort of stuff."

I begrudgingly attended an interview at a renowned company near my parents' house that specialised in cloths. "What can I say about cloths? I love and adore cloths. I'd be proud to sell such wonderful world-renowned cloths. In five years time? Hopefully still selling cloths."

I wasn't pulling the wool (or cloth) over anyone's eyes.

A saving grace would arrive in the unlikely form of landscape gardening. I was given a week-long trial with a local gardener. It was a scorching summer, so I was looking forward to working al-fresco and making a bit of money at the same time. As for experience, well I used to dig massive holes in the garden at our old house in West Linton for absolutely no reason. Granted, I was six-years-old, it was with a trowel, and there were no time constraints, but regardless I was sure I'd be a natural in this new environment.

Making sense of a spirit level, mixing concrete, putting up fences, strimming grass badly and falling off a van and tipping soil all over the road all added up to me not securing a second week at that job. "Thanks for trying, but I think we can both agree that you're not really cut out for manual labour are you?" my soon to be former boss proclaimed as he tore off a cheque and sent me on my way. I couldn't argue with that assertion.

Determined to make amends for my failed gardening exploits I unenthusiastically trudged around the centre of Edinburgh armed with CVs firing them like a t-shirt gun in the direction of any temping agency I could find. Temping agencies were a fine short-term solution but gave you as much security as jumping out of a plane without a parachute on a cloudy day with the constant fear you'd chin the concrete at any moment. I'd be quite happily plodding away in a job one day, then on the bus home get a call to say my contract had been terminated with no luxury of an explanation the next. It was a brutal wheel of fortune, but from my experience that appeared to be the norm and the attitude towards temporary workers in the mid-2000s.

A few soul-destroying months of temporary work at numerous banks and a stationary company ensued. To be fair, the latter wasn't the worst job I've ever had as I got a free lunch every day consisting of all you can eat Kit Kats and Diet Coke. The job itself was essentially just running up and down the stairs of the adjoining law firm to see if they needed any more pens and replenishing their paper and fruit bowls which incidentally may as well have contained plastic fruit because no one in the building seemed to consume anything other than free Kit Kats.

When I was fed up trying to pawn my services to countless longer-term employers with little to no joy, I began writing some songs. The first one I wrote was about a fictional ghost one of my friend's had told me she'd seen in her attic. I can't remember all of it, but it had a formidable chorus.

Ghosts in the Attic

Ghosts in the attic
I just cannot stand it
Don't know what to do, afraid a ghost will jump out and say boo
There's one in the attic
There's one by the door
Please say there ain't any more

I wrote quite a few in the space of a couple of weeks, including a song called 'Get a Job' which was a nod to my summer of discontent of trying and failing to land a job I could be proud of. I'd listened to a band called The Pigeon Detectives quite a lot the Summer, and they had a song called 'Take Her Back' which I basically ripped off the chorus from. I interviewed the band about ten years later for an online music blog and confessed I'd ripped their song off. They were lovely guys but didn't seem remotely bothered or in the least bit interested, so I took that as copyright clearance.

Get a Job

Hate my job but it pays the rent
A penny earned is a penny spent
Up at five every day of the week
And when I get home I just want to sleep they shout

Get a job, get a job, get a job, get a job, get a job, get a job today
Get a job, get a job, get a job, get a job, get a job, get a job today

Bus arrives at 6:25
Takes that long that I wish I could drive
Same faces in the same old seats
It's bad enough without having to hear

Get a job, get a job, get a job, get a job, get a job, get a job today
Get a job, get a job, get a job, get a job, get a job, get a job today

Down the corridors I always walk
I see people, but they never talk
Typing, typing, typing all day long, while I'm listening to Jing Jang Jong

Get a job, get a job, get a job, get a job, get a job, get a job today

Get a job, get a job, get a job, get a job, get a job, get a job today

Hate my job but it pays the rent
Hate my job but it pays the rent
Hate my job but it pays the rent

Jing Jang Jong was an obscure reference to a band I went to see a couple of times called Joe Lean & the Jing Jang Jong. A band I liked 90% because of their odd name and the singer's indie cheekbones. I particularly enjoyed telling people with a straight face that I liked a band with such an utterly ridiculous name. A renowned mistake I made at T in the Park one year was when I went to see them instead of The Stereophonics, presumably because once again I was confident it would make a hilarious story back in the campsite. And once again, It didn't.

Writing songs is an immensely personal thing and it can be incredibly hard to share them with others, particularly when it reveals an undiscovered fear of fictional ghosts. Like the ghost, that one unsurprisingly failed to make an appearance again.

After a few months of writing my own songs and half-arsed learning cover versions quietly so the neighbours wouldn't judge me, I felt ready to play my first proper gig. Sporting my newly acquired black hair, an oddly chosen black and white striped wristband, rosary beads which were purchased from the sacred land of H&M and a brown coloured t-shirt with the words 'James Brown says stay in school' on it (to this day I still don't understand the joke). I turned up three hours early for an open mic night at the Eastgate Theatre in Peebles and holed myself up in the dressing room beneath the stage on edge for the next few hours, unable to control my nerves at the prospect of having to play four songs in front of around twenty people, it was safe to say I was absolutely terrified. I'm attributing a lot of these nerves to the fact the dressing room had one of those mirrors designed only for famous folk, the ones surrounded by an unnecessary amount of lightbulbs. I was thinking 'Shit, lights around my mirror?! I'm only one blue bowl of M&M's away from fame.' My nerves didn't exactly improve when I got out on stage, and I proceeded to absolutely murder a cover of 'Albion' by Babyshambles, a song I'm pretty sure only one girl in the audience knew, but even she was visibly struggling with my interpretation. This wasn't a good start, in fact, the Scottish Borders hadn't witnessed as bad a start as this since my primary school sack race, but somehow I felt my mum running on and carrying me to the finish line this time might actually spare some of my blushes. 'Green Eyes' by Coldplay was up next on my list of songs that I successfully put the audience off for life. It was a song I had seen a few of my school friends perform well at the school's charity concert so I thought I'd be able to do it justice. Out of tune? Check. Forgot the words? Uh-huh. Stopped midway through from nerves and rather unfortunately extremely audibly mouthed the words "Oh for fuck's sake!" into the microphone which split the room with shock and muffled laughter as some in the audience tried and failed to deflect their laughter into the final oatcake left on their cheeseboard? Yup. After a horror show of a start, I finished with my song 'Change Your Ways.' A song I would continue to subject audiences to for the next seven or eight years.

Change Your Ways

New beginnings, different ways
Change your hairstyle, change your face
A different lifestyle, it all depends
If you don't like it you can always change your friends

Change your ways
Change your ways

All I wanted was to be alone
It's kind of hard when you are always on the phone

Change your ways
Change your ways

Live a new life and forget the past
If you don't then you might just grow up too fast
Live a new life and forget the past
If you don't then you might just grow up too fast

Change your ways
Change your ways

Choose your own direction
Don't listen to what others say
You could have things your own way
Choose your own direction

Don't listen to what others say
You could have things your own way

So change your ways

Change your ways
Change your ways
Change your ways

   The pressure lifted when I played that song, primarily because no one, other than myself, had heard it before so even if I did mess it up, everyone else in the room would be none the wiser.

   Despite such a poor self-assessment, once the shame wore off midway through a post-gig pint, I found solace in the fact that I'd made it out of that gig alive. If I went away and wrote more songs, I'd not be as bad next time—a logic I'd maintain for the next three or four gigs.

   My final foray in the world of temporary work was an office job with a well-known health service in the centre of the city. Rather than the usual couple of weeks, this one was dubbed as an ongoing contract with no end in sight. At first, this seemed like a golden opportunity, but it wasn't long until I was bored to tears. You know how before you could buy tickets on Ticketmaster back in the day you had to solve an infuriating captcha? For those of you that aren't familiar with them, a captcha is a blurred series of letters and numbers which don't make up a proper word and they're written in infuriatingly difficult to read text that you need to squint to see properly to prove that you're not a robot. Now imagine working for a year in a job where your sole purpose was to solve captchas all day, but the captchas were actually smudged and woefully written prescriptions and if you entered them incorrectly on the system you've probably logged someone's prescription wrong. On top of that, unlike with Ticketmaster there was no carrot in the form of tickets waiting at the other end, just an endless conveyor belt of illegible nonsense. Mind-numbing and repetitive as the job was, the staff were all harmless. Well, all apart from the livewire Johnny Cash impersonator who sat a row along from me. He would openly inform the staff of his lunchtime exploits. He wasn't a member of the highly popular cheese sandwich on stale bread whilst nose deep in the Metro newspaper brigade. For him, lunchtimes appeared to consist of one or more of the following; going to the pub, going to the bookies, or his monthly post-pay day treat of walking fifty or sixty yards to the lane round the corner, banging a hooker on a car bonnet then coming back to give the staff his rating out of ten. By contrast, my lunch would be a macaroni pie from Greggs or a pizza slice from an Italian café if I was feeling extravagant. The rest tended to keep themselves to themselves, so it was easy enough to go to work, plug in my iPod and switch off from my surroundings without having any real meaningful interactions.

I left that job when an opportunity arrived at Ripping Records, a ticket and CD shop in Edinburgh. This was a dream come true. Any time I was in Edinburgh, I'd spend hours on end shuffling through the racks, conversing with John and Nik behind the counter and screening the impressive handwritten chalk ticket board to see what I could spend what little money I had on. A perk of working there was I could go to practically any show I wanted to. Whilst I was shy at exploiting this at first, by the end of my time there I'd be going to easily three or four shows a week.

The nature of the role meant that although I still lacked in basic conversational skills, I was slowly learning to use the job to my advantage. Many of the local promoters and venue managers were in and out of the shop daily, so this would present an opportunity to convince them that I was good enough to play at their venue. The problem was that I didn't have any way of proving (or disproving) this. I needed a CD with recordings on it. I didn't have anything remotely resembling disposable income, so I wasn't able to afford the eye-watering studio costs to record what I had to admit were still largely unfinished and underdeveloped songs. Luckily, the sawdust in my wallet was safe as, by some minor miracle, the local Youth Action Group in Peebles were looking for acts to record and try out their new studio. I mustered the courage to ask, and they duly obliged by recording my first four-track demo.

I spent the day recording a four-track CD which I labelled 'The Wet Paint EP' on account of it still being a work in progress. 'Change Your Ways', 'Air Meets the Sky', 'Get a Job' and 'Jungle Assault' all made the cut, largely because those were the only four songs I had at my disposal at that point (if you discount 'Ghosts in the Attic' which wasn't going anywhere near a recording studio).

Whilst admittedly, it was a bit rushed, a bit all over the place and unlikely to get an airing on Radio 1, it was an incredible feeling to hold a copy of my first CD and a proud moment when I handed it over to my parents.

This was a huge turning point for my confidence, and I'd finally managed to dig myself out of a hole, something I can safely say I wouldn't have managed if I was still a landscape gardener.

Two days later, all of the songs were on my My-Space page and I began throwing out CDs like confetti at a wedding, though given the reaction from some, confetti at a funeral is probably a more accurate metaphor. Nobody was safe from my shameless and verging on violent plugging. I'd leave the CDs on racks in shops, hand them into venues and bars, and scribble my MySpace address (myspace.com/richardcobb-music, FYI) on the back of music publications that landed in the shop.

To subsidise the job at Ripping, I worked the rest of my week at The County Inn in Peebles. The County was the local haunt of many of Peebles up and coming wide-eyed wildlife. A few of the regulars there would often sit staring into space looking bored and utterly miserable. For that reason, I managed to fit right in.

College:

My previous brief peer through the keyhole at a college had all but put me off the whole experience for good. Prior to attending Napier, I'd gone to an open day at a fairly notorious college in Edinburgh for an insight into their Events Management course. I had a firm idea in my mind that the events I wanted to put on were music and music only. The day basically consisted of the course organiser condescendingly telling me that music was an extremely difficult area to break into, so their course mainly focused on catering which had "more realistic career opportunities." I took a wide berth on that, but the experience left me slightly deflated and justifiably cautious of a repeat experience of that shitshow. That would change when I saw a flyer for a Music Business course at a local college on a shelf at the shop. The clue was in the title that this wasn't going to focus on cheap icing, distracting young offenders, and lowering self-esteem.

I applied for a place on the two-year HND course, and

a few months later I'd be attending Jewel and Esk College in what would be a somewhat life-affirming experience. This meant jacking in the job at Ripping to focus on the full-time course, which was bittersweet. As much as I enjoyed my time at the shop, there were undeniably times of intense boredom when we had no customers and all I'd do was gaze at the attractive blonde hairdressers in the Polish barbershop across the road, read the back of every CD in the shop, dust, eat scones or occasionally run outside with a bottle of Volvic to put out the smoke from the bin that would frequently catch fire from ill-judged cigarettes outside and waft in through the open door of the shop.

Still, the way music sales were going, it was evident there wasn't going to be a sustainable career for me working a few days a week in the shop, and I couldn't justify spending roughly a third of my wages on transport. Was I any more likely to bag a job at the end of a two-year college course? I didn't know the answer to that, but there was only one way to find out.

I packed my things into my 21st Birthday present, a white Mazda my mum and dad bought me. Thomas (you're lying if you say you've never named your car) had a Newcastle United sticker on the back window that said 'Shear Quality' in reference to their former striker Alan Shearer and a small saltire on the boot. I drove an hour up the road to my new digs. Actually, that's not entirely true. I made it to the outskirts of Edinburgh then pulled into a layby and handed the wheel over to my mum to finish the journey as she was clearly terrified by my experimental driving style "Sixty's only a suggestion! You don't actually need to drive that fast!" was the memorable line from that day.

Oh yeah, did I mention I'd managed to pass my driving test by then? Like my theory test, it was third time lucky for my practical test before I was let loose on the tarmac.

College was the best thing that could happen to me at that time. In the years preceding my enrolment on the Music Business course, I'd regularly send myself into a tailspin whenever I spent more than a couple of seconds pondering my future career path. A two year HND course not only deferred that unanswerable question, it also set me on my way to realising that when I put my mind to it, I was actually capable of working hard and crucially retaining knowledge when tasked with necessary coursework. It turns out all it took was a subject I was passionate about, and the rest pieced itself together. I was completely immersed in every aspect of the course. Recording contracts, learning how to hold events, working with a band in the studio, marketing, music videos, influencing on social media and copyright laws. I lapped it all up, and it brought fascinating insight and valuable experience on an industry I'd held close to my heart for so long. My success in the course was in no small part down to the care and support from my lecturers Mike and Paul. They had a perfect balance of making the course content fun and engaging whilst also injecting their real-life experiences from the industry into the coursework to help guide us into getting a foot in the door and finding our way in a fairly full-on and unforgiving industry. Mike clearly held back on divulging the full extent of his Mötley Crüe-esque heyday, but he certainly had a story or two to tell about the time he spent in a touring band.

Living in the student accommodation adjacent to the college was perfect as I could stumble out of bed at five to nine and still arrive on time for morning classes. My new surroundings also helped build confidence when meeting the hordes of new people I was lodging with. This meant that when I started going to more gigs, my chat was less forced which in turn led to getting decent contacts from bands and promoters and that helped when it came to putting on my own nights further down the line. I was still nervous and no stranger to waffling on incoherently to unamused strangers (a lot like what I'm doing now) but the more I subjected myself to these awkward social interactions, the less of an ordeal it became over time.

One afternoon before a gig we were hosting for a band in the college auditorium, we were getting the stage set up when I got a call from my sister Gemma to tell me that my grandpa Cobb had taken a bad turn at the hospital and I should get down there as quickly as I could. With the bus connection taking well over an hour, I nervously hopped in my car. Truth be told I was petrified of driving in the city centre as up until then I'd mostly travelled back and forth to Peebles via the outskirts of Edinburgh and onto the city Bypass which aside from one nightmare roundabout was a reasonably routine drive. Seeing the bigger picture and putting my fear to the side, I drove across town to the hospital.

The rest is a bit of a blur. I remember seeing my grandpa one last time that night and not really knowing what to do with that thought. Up until then I hadn't been faced with a death in the family, aside from when I was maybe two and far from compos mentis enough to realise what was going on. I was heartbroken when Corrie our Golden Retriever died back in Fergusson View and when my fish or one of my sisters' rabbits would die, I'd feel a great deal of sadness at the time. Ultimately though, there was always a feeling that eventually, life went on and that death was a learning curve we all had to experience at some stage in life. This hit much harder and was so much more difficult to process.

I stayed over at the family home the following evening as I had back to back shifts working at The County. I remember being woken up in the middle of the night by a hug from my mum when she broke the news to me that my grandpa had passed away. I'd fully anticipated the news to arrive sooner or later, and I'd tried my hardest to prepare myself as best I could, but it all felt so surreal and impossible to put into words. The overwhelming sadness came from seeing the rest of the family's grief, and I still find that the hardest thing to deal with when faced with a loss. I feel bad that I haven't written more about him in these books. He was a tremendous man whose larger than life stories of wild nights spent in Edinburgh's Harry's Bar, watching Hearts away in Europe, time spent in Oman and proudly captaining Gullane golf club were only exceeded by his love for his family.

As with the tough lessons learnt with the passing of pets earlier in life, even when it feels impossible to come to terms with grief, there's something important to remember. When the family all pull together to help each other through, if you look hard enough, there's always a break in the clouds where the light eventually starts to creep in. From then on you can begin to look at things in a more positive light and think just how lucky you've been to have had those great people in your life and those moments to cherish and fondly look back on.

To begin with, when I moved to Edinburgh to start college, I continued to commute back and forth a few nights a week and at weekends to work at the bar. It didn't take long to realise it was all a bit of a faff for a job that brought little reward aside from a few standard off-target attempts at trying to woo some of my colleagues with my glass cleaning and pint pouring ability.

On a day off from the bar, Valentine's Day 2010 to be exact, my car met its unfortunate demise. Colliding with another vehicle at the junction of Edinburgh's Ferry Road and Great Junction Street. I'm not going to lay blame at anyone's doorstep (it was 100% them and their shitey wee Renault). By the age of twenty-one, I'd had my fair share of metaphorical car crashes on Valentine's Day, but this was the first literal one. You'd think panic would be the first thing to cross your mind in the opening few seconds after an accident. Not me, I was too caught up in the horror that I was listening to King Creosote at the point of impact and that whining bastard would be my car's final memory. Poor guy (the car, not King Creosote). I'd always envisaged going out in something triumphant like 'Born in the USA' by Springsteen or that tune from Peter and the Wolf. If I could change two things about that crash, it would be first and foremost, firing King Creosote out the window and right into the Water of Leith at the earlier traffic lights and secondly, not crashing.

Seeing off the car at the scrapyard with my dad was a sad moment and one I felt incredibly vexed about. As you can surmise, I'm sentimental at the best of times, but leaving behind the car my mum and dad had lovingly bought me for my 21st less than a year before was a sore one. On the bright side, I'd managed to sidestep another near-death experience thanks to the Herculean strength of my first car (coupled with the fact I was going about 10mph when I crashed).

As the car was now out of the equation, it was clear I could no longer juggle living and studying in Edinburgh and commuting back a few nights a week to Peebles for my bar job. I had no option but to call it quits. I was a little downbeat because I got on well with the staff there, but for the most part, it was an overwhelming sigh of relief to be able to draw a line under the late-night commutes and leave behind what remained of the ever-diminishing Peebles social scene.

Rock Star Pt II:

The Voodoo Rooms, Edinburgh, 2010 (ish).

Spending more time in Edinburgh allowed me to gig more frequently across a myriad of venues. My college lecturers were incredibly supportive too and would encourage me to go out and play as many gigs as I could, even if it meant I'd sometimes need to dip out of class early to travel to a gig. I'd hop between a mixed bag of open mic nights often playing a few open mics across the city on the same evening. I'd quickly learn that whilst some were exhilarating and brought enthusiastic crowds; a vast majority would be an absolute train wreck and a scene right out of Ricky Gervais' *Life on the Road*.

One night I played a pub near my old flat in Gorgie. I'd tried and failed to get a gig there a few years previously when I lived around the corner, so it felt like a small if somewhat begrudging achievement to be able to finally tick that one off the list.

When setting up, I overheard a table of six guys at the back of the room letting out a collective sigh at the sight of an acoustic guitarist setting up in the corner of the bar. It was a sigh I could empathise with given that it was and still is my chosen reaction when faced with a similar mood killer. "Oh, here we go, bet this guy will be doing fucking Coldplay covers" one of them audibly quipped to the rest of the group. Now, I hadn't intended to play any Coldplay songs that night because I'd gone off them a bit by then and more importantly it was a Monday night and everyone in there already seemed sufficiently depressed. However, having already turned up with a slight chip on my shoulder given my previous rejection and now being faced with a potentially tricky crowd, I plugged in, trundled over to the microphone, introduced myself and said, "I'm going to play a few of my songs for you tonight, but first up here's a Coldplay cover." No sooner had my plectrum connected with the strings when the group of six downed their pints in unison and scurried out of the bar unamused. Having successfully halved the attendance in the bar with a single strike of a chord I played a few more to mild, potentially sarcastic applause before packing my bag, taking a few sips of a flat pint of Tennents (my generous payment for the gig) and catching a bus back across town.

Another memorable for all the wrong reasons gig was an in-store performance at a clothes shop in the St Enoch Centre in Glasgow. It was the first time I'd been asked to perform an in-store show, so naturally, I felt like my stock was rising and my MySpace page views (which incidentally were primarily made up from shamelessly refreshing my own page at any given opportunity) would skyrocket by the end of the night. As I would be performing in a clothing store, I thought long and hard about my costume choice for the evening so I wasn't upstaged by a trendy mannequin. I went with a blue and white striped long sleeve t-shirt, black jeans and finished the look off with a maroon Hearts scarf. Hearts had narrowly beaten Celtic the night before in a cagey midweek affair, so my spirits were high, and I foolishly harboured no fear whatsoever about my bold choice of neckwear.

Sitting backstage (behind the curtain of the store's only changing room), I was told I could start to play. I had slight reservations about this request as I didn't know where I was meant to stand and there was nobody in the shop aside from myself and the member of staff. "Awch as thur's naebdy here ye can jist like sort eh wunder aboot wae yir guitar an that" she suggested in her thick as treacle Glaswegian accent. I took her advice and played a few songs whilst doing laps of the shop. I'm not sure where I stand with people walking and playing guitar at the same time. It feels like the guitar equivalent of cycling with no hands on the handlebars. As it would transpire, I was dreadful at both. Every so often someone would wander in, clock me and either go to the opposite end of the store or swivel around and back out the store again like a standing reverse version of the TV show *The Voice*. After six or seven songs, the owner told me she was probably going to shut the shop for the night as the shopping centre was "unusually dead for a Thursday." This news was unequivocally the highlight of my night.

Luckily, I wouldn't have many worse gigs than that one, but one night in St Andrews ran it close in terms of the sheer awkwardness I once again found myself in. I'd been invited up to support a band at The Freshers Week having met them a month or so before at a show in Edinburgh. The gig itself was amazing and possibly up there with one of my favourites. There were a few hundred crammed into the venue I was playing in, and thanks to the miracle of alcohol, people seemed responsive to the songs. Having a few celebratory drinks afterwards with the band we decided to drop our guitars off at their flat where I was staying that night and headed across the road to the student union to see a Radio 1 DJ. Arriving at the door of the Union, a bouncer informed me only St Andrews Uni students were allowed in. The band apologised and quite rightly went in to enjoy themselves leaving me to traipse off back to their empty flat alone to sit in my room for the night until I was tired enough to go to sleep. On reflection, I could have probably just gone back to the first venue to enjoy the rest of the night, but the thought somehow never crossed my mind as I sat in silence bored off my tits. Still, the gig itself was phenomenal, and Vernon Kay was probably shite anyway.

It'll sound ridiculous but even the truly awful and at times unbearably awkward gigs are great to look back on. From playing a festival in the Borders in some posh farmer's back garden to travelling down to London alone on a Tuesday night to play Camden's historic Dublin Castle are experiences that I'm proud to have had. The solo music career didn't quite pan out as I'd hoped, but I gave it a bloody good go. I played as much as was physically possible, had loyal support from family and friends who would often come down to my Edinburgh shows, and I had a great laugh in the process even if that sometimes meant at my own expense. All of the above made it all worthwhile and a memorable adventure.

The Cinema:

With my bar job down the pan I was determined to continue down the path of self-sufficiency (aside from the accommodation and food costs- thanks mum and dad!) more so than I was at university. I fired off a few CVs to local pubs and restaurants in the hope of tying down some much-needed part-time work to fund my extra-curricular activities (predominantly Pop-Tarts and beer).

Alongside my college friends, John and Rob, I quickly landed a job at a popular cinema chain not too far down the road in Leith. I won't name the cinema for legal reasons, so let's just call them something imaginative like 'View Cinemas.'

It was a thirty-hour a week contract which meant I could get a steady flow of money in and on top of that I could get into films for free. I was no longer the film buff that I had been in high school when I longed to remake *Lord of the Rings*, but it was still a role I was pretty enthusiastic about.

There were four main roles which would be divided amongst the staff for a weekly rota, concessions, Ben & Jerry's, floor/barrier and box office. Concessions was without a shadow of a doubt my least favourable aspect of the job. Serving tickets and food on a Friday or Saturday night was gruelling. It was ten times worse on a Sunday morning when coupled with an unapologetic hangover, there was the added brain dynamite of having to contend with £1 kids screens which would house 300 kids and their equally hungover and short of patience parents.

Most parents would make the irrecoverable mistake of succumbing to their poltergeist's demands and plying them with copious amounts of sugar to appease them, the equivalent of giving a gremlin a glass of water or pouring petrol on a bonfire.

There was a slight reprieve from the lions outside in the kitchen and stock room area around the back of the concessions stand. It had a faulty camera which meant we could have a bit of a breather and lie down on the fridges or wolf down a few nachos which didn't pass our strict self-diagnosed quality control.

The floor shifts were where some of the most memorable parts of the job took place. Covering the barrier meant you'd be 10% in charge of checking tickets and directing customers to their screens and 90% in charge of telling wave after wave of hard of hearing American tourists that we weren't the bloody Royal

Yacht Britannia. The Britannia was located at the opposite end of the shopping centre, the sea end to be exact. Not overlooking the road where they had just moments earlier piled off their bus with their matching cargo shorts and cameras. Actually, while I'm on the topic of that boat, I vividly remember one old boy charging past me and straight up the escalators like he was ascending the travellator on *Gladiators.* Arriving at the peak, he cast his eyes out the window expecting to see the Queen's old yacht. The disappointment was written all over his face when he found out I wasn't lying to him about him being in a cinema, not a vessel that once belonged to Queen Elizabeth II and he'd bust a gut up the escalators to set eyes on nothing more than the barren wasteland overlooking the shopping centre. That was a sublime day.

One typically busy Sunday morning I was at the barrier awaiting the usual onslaught of parents and kids charging up the escalators to the weekly kids screening when I noticed the queue at the concessions stand trailing back halfway across the foyer. Unusually, nobody was being served at the Ben & Jerry's stand. With time being of the essence and not long until the film started, I decided I'd be the hero of the hour and announce that they could also get tickets and food at the Ben & Jerry's counter. This would ease the pressure of the concessions staff and lessen the chance of anyone missing the start of whatever old shite we were charging £1 for that weekend. Clearing my throat to ensure I didn't go high pitched in front of a hall full of people I momentarily abandoned my post at the barrier and marched to the middle of the foyer with purpose. "Excuse me, hello, excuse me," I uttered confidently like some sort of rich messiah who had revealed themselves at the last minute just in time to save a block of flats from an impending demolition in a rotten and predictable film. The parents turned around like well-oiled meerkats and glared in the direction of their mysterious saviour. "You can also get served at..." my good deed was brought to an abrupt end. As I turned around to point at the vacant Ben & Jerry's queue, a running child collided chin-first on my knee and went sliding face-first across the immaculately shiny floor of the foyer. "Eeehh. Over there by the ice cream stand" my voice going high as I brought the whole crowd to a standstill. Thankfully, the boy got up seconds later, seemingly unfazed (probably because of the concussion). I sheepishly trudged back to the barrier to await an onslaught of disapproving tutting from parents. Oddly, nobody seemed to give nearly as much of a shit about it as I did. The onslaught passed me by without even a single reference to my public guillotining of a small child.

Long stints covering the barrier were incredibly monotonous, and there wasn't much to do when the place was quiet aside from occasionally sweeping popcorn off the floor or drifting over to concessions to chat to colleagues. One day I was particularly bored and started doodling on a sheet of paper with the film times on it. The film *Wrath of the Titans* had just been released so for whatever reason I drew a picture of one of my colleagues Karl Raasch in the lead role and titled it 'Wrath of the Karl.' As with most things in life, I took this fairly uneventful incident too far, and this would become a regular feature. 'We Bought a Karl,' 'Karls on a Plane,' Anna Karlenina,' 'The Woman in Karl,' and 'Karl Fishing in the Yemen' all followed in quick succession. At one stage, Karl had been my archnemesis as we were both competing head to head in a site-wide competition one Christmas to see who could sell the most gift cards. The winner would receive an HD USB video camera. I had no real use for such an object, but I was every bit as determined to beat Karl as he was to beat me. In the end, after a closely fought battle, I was victorious and won the camera. I insisted Karl present me with it at our next team meeting. A wickedly petty move and one I wasn't proud of, but it was a move I had no doubt Karl would have similarly exploited had the shoe been on the other foot. I think the camera's in my parents' attic now and I'd only used it once to film a stand-up set which went down horribly. As for the Karl drawings, I continue to send them to him over Facebook every year on his birthday. Recent new additions include 'Juraaschic Park,' 'Three Karls Outside Ebbing, Missouri,' 'Karley Quinn,' and my most recent effort going slightly off-topic, 'The Karlona virus.'

The infamous Karl drawings.

I enjoyed the freedom of the floor shift as most of the time when not covering the barrier you could spread your wings and drift between screens avoiding people. It was also an opportunity to have a good laugh/rant with your colleagues whilst cleaning the screens for the next showing, or risk your life by taking the bins down in the rickety old service lift to the ground floor. The job was a bit of a revolving door, particularly over busy periods like school holidays, people left, and others started every few weeks, so it was sometimes difficult to keep track of everyone you worked alongside.

In the Summer of 2011, I successfully graduated from college, and a couple of weeks later, Sara started working at the cinema. As usual with the new starts, I barely said a word to her on her first shift when we were cleaning screens together. The day things changed a little was one memorable morning when she arrived at work with a massive hangover. The days when someone else suffers from a monumental hangover always make you appreciate the fact you don't have one so much more. Schadenfreude aside, I remember that day vividly as, though she was clearly struggling and didn't need me nagging in her ear, we were talking quite a bit and the conversation was flowing rapidly, much like her vodkas and Jägerbombs the night before. We spent more time together on nights out and occasionally saw a few films together in a group, but I was in a relationship at the time, and I didn't think she was in the least bit interested. Everything carried on as it was for a few months until it was clear things were blossoming and we were becoming more than friends. (Before I go any further I'd just like to apologise at this point. Given the dark and gloomy cover and my glorious failure in the previous book, you haven't knowingly picked up this book thinking it was going to turn full rom-com. I imagine right now you're sat there thinking, 'blossoming? Pass the sick bag!' Don't worry, there's plenty more peril lurking just around the corner.) Having recently parted ways with my girlfriend at the time, Sara and I began seeing each other and things (aside from the couple times I self-sabotaged things in the early years) have been amazing ever since.

I'll be the first to admit that working in a cinema wasn't the most glamorous job in the land and there were times I'd be bored out of my mind, but it served its purpose alongside studying and the nights out were legendary.

The Hive was the post-work establishment of choice. During the week it was free entry and you could get a soapy vodka coke and most likely an STD for the very reasonable sum of £1. £10 nights out, if executed well, were a thing of beauty. Unlike working in the cinema, to survive a night in The Hive you'd need to utilise your brain. It was important to consume just the right amount of watered-down alcohol to make you comfortable with your surroundings and lifestyle choices. It was equally important not to peak too soon or you'd run out of money and sober up in a room full of sweaty goths listening to Alien Ant Farm and Papa Roach without any reasonable explanation. Leaving before the lights came on at 3 am was also advisable otherwise you'd instantly sober up when surveying the post-apocalyptic carnage that lay before you. The few times I wasn't successfully out the door by 3 am were the closest I'd get to experiencing the horrors of war. Bodies were strewn across every crevice of the cavernous venue, sick everywhere, sweat on the walls and an intense feeling of regret from everyone in attendance. Post-Hive guilt was a common diagnosis for the cinema staff and usually written on the faces of a good third of the staff members on any given day. The fact the stamps took the best part of an hour to wash off meant most would turn up with their trophies still emblazoned on their wrists the morning after. "You'll never guess where I ended up last night" was frequently delivered with faux-regret and a side smile. The reality was that almost everyone loved their nights out there and the closeness of the staff (I mean that in every sense of the word- the place made *Love Island* look like a convent) was unlike any other job I'd experience, even if they wouldn't openly admit it.

Sara and I's first photo together. The Hive, 2011.

Throughout my time at the cinema, I'd been living

in a variety of flats with John (of college and cinema fame). To begin with, it was at the college accommodation, then in a flat with him, Rob, and my old college neighbour Callum on Leith Walk. In that flat, I'd spend the best part of a year staying in a miserable windowless room with a sofa bed that when unfurled took up the whole circumference of the room. As the lease agreement stipulated that there was only meant to be three people living in the property, we had a carefully constructed plan. Each time the letting agency carried out their routine inspection, we'd fill the room with coats and football boots so it resembled a storage cupboard (it didn't take much effort to pull off this Superman to Clark Kent transition). While I'm on the topic of films, if Harry Potter had found himself subjected to that place he'd have fucked off to Hogwarts with his owl long before he did when he was living the life of Riley in his bachelor pad under his dead mum's sister's staircase. Still, my rent was something like £80 a month, so I couldn't really complain. After a year, John and I abandoned the flock and moved to a new flat which was a massive upgrade on the last cesspit.

The old crew (L-R) Rob, Callum, me and John. The Hive, 2010 (ish).

One year John was in a terrible state around Christmas without shedding any light on the reasons why he was acting like a bigger dick than usual. I did what any caring friend and flatmate would do. I let him suffer in silence and made no attempt to question the source of his issues. After a few months, his mood miraculously picked up, like some sort of R.E.M. transition from 'Everybody Hurts' to 'Shiny Happy People.' He opened up that the reason he wasn't himself was that he thought he'd inadvertently impregnated a girl he met at a bus stop late the previous year. It was a false alarm as it transpired that she'd lied to him and wasn't pregnant. Now, obviously, in reality, this is a very serious situation for any young person to have to deal with and if he'd opened up about it, I'd like to think I'd offer him some sort of low-level emotional support for a few minutes. However, in the context of a flat where the words too far and decorum didn't exist, I had an absolute field day here.

For his birthday a few months after the revelations, I presented him with a used Biffy Clyro ticket that I'd been using as a bookmark and a set of condom instructions. I didn't wrap it, but I think the failure to wrap formed the basis of my joke. There wasn't really a point to this story, and he'll probably annihilate me if I leave this bit in the book. That said, if John has taught me anything over our ten plus years of friendship, it's his narrowly unblemished ethos of just stick it in there and worry about any negative repercussions later.

One morning I got up and put my customary navy blue dressing gown on, swung open my bedroom door and fell face-first over some sort of contraption that I can only assume belonged on a film set. I knew little about the ins and outs of a film set, but I assumed this belonged on one because there just so happened to be a whole film crew spread out across my flat. 'Oi, be careful, that's expensive!' I heard someone snarl from somewhere amongst a crowd of people in questionable outfits. My initial reaction to this scene of confusion was that John had sub-letted our flat to some young aspiring gay porn director. "Oh, morning mate, yeah you know that "small film" I said might get shot in the living room? Yeah well, quite a lot more people turned up than I thought. Hope you don't mind." John said calmly. I was livid. Why? I'm not sure, but regardless of the cause of my disgruntlement, I was still visibly furious at this invasion of wankers. As silence fell across the flat, I fought my way through the crowd to get a cup of coffee and a bowl of granola. Just as I began boiling the kettle, I heard a sharp "Excuse me. Quiet please" erupt from the living room as though delivered by an umpire and my flat had been magically transformed into the Centre Court at Wimbledon. I stomped out of the kitchen and politely served back "Sorry mate, I actually live here and, well the thing is I actually don't have a clue who you are or what you're doing in my flat. So, if it's alright with you, I'm just going to pour myself a coffee then fuck off back to my room where there's none of you and no cameras." "Oh eh. Sorry sure eh yeah no problem" he responded with his tail between his legs. Walking back through the newly parted sea of people in my dressing gown like a victorious Moses, I arrived back to the comfort of my room and thought to myself' All things considered, I actually think I handled that pretty well.' Just as I put down my coffee down on the side table, I managed to trip over a loose cable and proceeded to lose grip of my ginormous bowl of granola complete with an overly-excessive serving of milk as it flew right into the eyes of my extension cable. I didn't bother going back out to grab another bowl.

Nightmare.

I've no idea what became of that film. A small part of me hopes it did well, but a large part of me hopes it nosedived like my bowl of granola.

Admittedly I've not exactly given John a sparkling critique in the last few anecdotes, but when he wasn't renting the place out to obnoxious gay porn directors, he was a cracking flatmate over the years.

I made friends for life at Vu.. I mean View, and it will forever be the place I met Sara. For that, I owe so much to the company.

The Bank Job:

When I eventually left the cinema at the tail end of 2012, I had a job at a bank for a couple of years. That revelation is probably nowhere near as exciting as the title 'The Bank Job' would suggest. Imagine after my stint at the cinema I'd suddenly unearthed my true calling, and in the months that followed, I was looting banks up and down the country for a living. I won't namecheck said bank I worked at because I probably blindly signed something once that said I couldn't talk about them in a book in any way, shape or form regardless of how low the readership is. Let's just say its title alluded to the fact it was a slightly more regal version of a bank of Scottish origin.

My workplace was a gigantic three-storey building plonked in the middle of a business park out the West of Edinburgh. Imagine *Charlie and the Chocolate Factory* if the chocolate and sweets were replaced with phones and broken dreams. Occasionally I'd walk past what I could have sworn was an Oompa Loompa in the staff canteen. On closer inspection, I would discover that it was merely a small girl from West Lothian that worked in the Customer Service team. I can only assume she must have inadvertently fallen face-first into the strong and unforgiving current of fake tan that ran through the heart of the county.

The start of any new job is a soul-destroying experience, and this one was no different. There was no shortage of icebreakers in my first week with other fresh-faced new starters. I can understand the boardroom logic behind the common icebreaker, so the newbies aren't too overwhelmed by their new surroundings, but by Christ, they're a terrible experience to live through. I've never taken to them, and I can't imagine anyone can solemnly say they enjoy any aspect of them. The painfully slow & wickedly awkward hospital waiting room-like encounter by the posh chairs at the reception area of a new job is surely punishment enough. Sharing a "fun fact" about yourself whilst working in groups of three to poorly assemble a block of Lego into a superhero for reasons which are never fully disclosed doesn't really break the ice, if anything it drops the temperature even more. Worse still, when you're split into groups and tasked with a problem-solving exercise. After getting a brain stitch trying to figure out the correct answer they smugly inform you "there's no right or wrong answer, it's just a fun little exercise." Fun my arse, I was dying to know our fate when escaping a sinking ship on a raft armed with nothing but a flare gun, a compass, and a packet of biscuits between five of us.

At the risk of driving this chapter off a cliff and reincarnating it as an extension of a dull LinkedIn bio, I started life at the bank as a 'Financial Crime Associate.' Actually, before I unpack that, Jesus Christ LinkedIn's dull isn't it? There's an astronomical amount of shameless peacocking from all angles. On Instagram people flaunt their flesh for attention, on LinkedIn they ram their IQs and made up motivational stories down your throat. Someday people will look back at the language used on LinkedIn in the same way I look back on the lingo kicking about in Shakespearean times. Pompous, convoluted, and deeply unnecessary. On every form of social media, whether it be Instagram or LinkedIn you're creating a version of yourself that's probably a million miles away from your real self. You could argue you do the same on a CV, but it just feels so much worse when you're subconsciously morphing into what you think represents an ideal version of yourself that others want to you to be, rather than just being your everyday self.

So yeah, Financial Crime Associate. Sounds terrifically exciting, doesn't it? Like something one of the sharp-dressed, effortlessly cool cigar smokers and verging on problem whisky drinkers from American TV shows *The Wire* or *Suits* would do in between looking so disgustingly well-groomed. The title was nearly as misleading as that of a 'Sandwich Artist' at Subway. A Sandwich Artist? Imagine Pablo Picasso pouring his heart and soul into meticulously dishing out olives and salami to a Hearty Italian to create one of his lauded Sub's of the Day. Each one would take him a solid twelve hours to craft into his own signature style. People would flock from all over in an attempt to snap up one of the two £2.49 Subs he managed to turn over each day. An honourable man, Picasso wouldn't let those in the queue that missed out go home empty-handed. He'd march up and down the queue signing Subway branded napkins with Chipotle Southwest sauce, then divide up the last remaining twelve-inch 9-Grain Honey Oat that, unless famine calls, nobody touches with a bargepole into two hundred equal pieces like a Spanish Jesus. One of the finest Sandwich Artists of our time.

Bullshit cloaks off, my job at the bank could be more accurately described as call centre worker and a Sandwich Artist, someone that makes sandwiches with as much signature as a painting by numbers artist. Still, no arguments that Financial Crime Associate and Sandwich Artist look bloody magnificent on a LinkedIn profile.

I'd take somewhere in the region of 80-100 calls a day dealing with fraud on debit cards. For the first few years I worked a fairly unforgiving shift of 10 am- 8 pm Tuesday, Wednesday, Friday and Saturday. It was pretty soul-destroying given I had to talk to angry bastards for ten hours straight. Actually, it was more like eight and a half hours out with breaks, but even that was pretty torturous. There weren't many highlights in the early days of that job due to the high demands and low tolerance of customers who were incensed that we stopped their card to check it was really them that was trying to buy a ninety-grand car or gold bullion, which until then I thought only existed in films with drug dealers or bank robbers. It's weird that money can drive people from having absolutely no shame to suddenly having bucket loads of it when their card suddenly gets declined for a perfectly valid security check. There were some perks though; it was always a good laugh when some tortured soul would call up in a panic the morning after they'd kicked the arse out of it on a heavy stag-do. With seemingly no knowledge of why a grand had left their account the night before, the memories would come flooding back quicker than last night's tequilas when informing them it was spent in a strippers or a massage parlour. They'd normally plead innocence and say someone must have stolen their card. By this point it was check-mate. "The transactions were done through chip & pin actually sir, so if you've still got your card on you and you haven't shared your pin with anyone, then it's most likely been you so there's not a lot we can do I'm afraid." Deafening silence ensued as I delivered my final verdict. "Oh... right" It was then you could hear the full weight of the hangover roundhouse kicking the guy in the face on the other end of the phone. Don't get me wrong, there's nothing remotely enjoyable about anyone having fraud com-

mitted against them, and in certain cases, it was brutal and really unpleasant to break the news to more
vulnerable members of society. But when it was a
simple case of a guy going on a massive bender and
pissing his money up a wall on WKD and chlamydia
with no hint of fraud it was it was an absolute day
maker.

To begin with, I'd be a bit melodramatic on the
phones when someone steamrolled me. I'd go maroon
in the face and probably throw my headset (I wore a
headset to answer the phones- this is neither exciting nor ground-breaking content, but I hadn't mentioned it earlier so felt I should do the decent thing
and address it in case anyone thought up until now
that I had to risk a serious repetitive strain injury by
manually picking up a phone 80-100 times each day)
on the floor, maybe even let out an unexpected rage
tear (normally only reserved for Hearts conceding a
late goal) once in a blue moon if I was feeling particularly perturbed by a foul-mouthed tirade. Over
time though I grew to quite enjoy people losing their
minds at me on the phone. It sounds quite masochis-
tic, but there was something oddly liberating about
it as there would inevitably be a turning point in the
call where the person on the other end would realise
that they've been a bit of a dick or that by continuing
their verbal machine-gunning wouldn't really solve
anything. It's like what Sun Tzu said in *The Art of War*,
'If you simply allow someone to give you a bollocking
without showing any sign of emotion or resistance,

eventually they'll get bored, fuck off and leave you alone.' It's been a while since I've read *The Art of War* so I may have ad-libbed there slightly.

Alongside a somewhat lethargic approach to job hunting, the social side of the job was probably one of the main reasons I stayed at the place for almost four years. It didn't quite rival the cinema for sheer off the scale debauchery, but it wasn't far off it at times. The one-two punch of a Friday and Saturday night out at Bar Salsa in the Grassmarket or some other wee shitey place we frequented in nearby Bread Street rewarded me with some colossally brutal hangovers.

In March or April of 2014, I joined up with my manager and a few colleagues for our usual routine of post-work pints. I wasn't really feeling it that night, probably because I had an earlier than usual start the following day, so I was clock watching for the little time I was there. With whispers of a club on the cards I decided to duck out early and walk back from a pub in the West End to my Leith flat. Walking along George Street at a brisk pace I crossed a zebra crossing onto the middle landing of Frederick Street. As I walked out onto the second set of zebra crossings at the other side of the street, I saw a black cab approach the crossing from the roundabout on the adjoining George Street. Being halfway across I did the universal sign of meekly waving 'thanks' to acknowledge the oncoming vehicle allowing me to cross safely. Only this time, something went horribly wrong. Rather

than slowing down, the taxi kept going at unrelent-
ing pace towards me. I could run through what was
going through my mind at that point, but to be honest, as much as I normally plan an exit strategy in
every eventuality, this sort of thing wasn't exactly a
common occurrence, so I was entirely focused on the
situation that was about to unfold. By this point, I
was some three-quarters of the way across the road,
so I had little option but to accept my fate. I managed
to jump just in time and take the brunt of the impact with my left knee as I connected with the bonnet of the moving vehicle which thankfully belatedly
slammed on the brakes as I slid off the bonnet hands
first onto the cold Edinburgh concrete. Unsurprisingly, you're visited by a wide array of unpleasant
emotions and confusion in the immediate aftermath
of being sconed by a fast-moving taxi. Firstly what
ran through my mind was 'What the actual fuck
just happened?' quickly followed by 'I better not be
dead because this is a really rubbish way to go' and
thirdly, and perhaps the most overpowering thought
of all 'Christ that's embarrassing, I hope nobody saw.'
Slowly getting to my feet I was met by a chorus of
gasps from one side of the road and playground laughter from the other like a split allegiance pantomime
audience. In any other country in the world, there
would surely be appropriate levels of concern from
passers-by. Trust my country of birth to respond to
an accident with ill-timed unstifled laughter.

I promptly went round to the driver's window to

quiz him on what had happened. He shakily informed me that he hadn't seen me and apologised profusely before offering to drive me somewhere. The brief ride on the bonnet was more than enough, there was no chance I was getting in that guy's taxi! Apologising once more, he drove off. The cab behind him stopped, and the driver got out to check I was OK. I felt good as new, aside from the fact my knee felt a bit sore, and my hands were a little grazed on impact. On reflection, the adrenaline, coupled with a mild serving of shock from the whole thing, probably gave me the false impression that everything was roses. He told me to report it to the police, who were a little further down the road. I spoke to them and gave a statement. Not wishing to take up any more of their time on a busy Friday night I refused a lift back and carried on walking my two-mile journey back. I called Sara on my way back to tell her what had happened, and she suggested I go to hers, which was probably a mile closer. It was only on the walk back that the severity of the event had hit me (unexpectedly, much like the taxi) 'What if the driver hadn't stopped? I could have been run over.' 'What if I'd landed on my head?' 'I'm certain there was nothing I could have done to avoid that, but what if it was my fault?' Lots of grim reflections unhelpfully swimming around my brain. I continued my journey back to Sara's with my thoughts going 100 miles an hour and my legs going about 1 mile an hour as the pain began to surface. Using the wall for leverage to slide up the stairway to Sara's flat, I got in and sat down on the sofa. Releasing my knee from its skinny jean captors to assess the damage, I found it had ballooned, and my wrists were starting to hurt, so after Sara called NHS 24 we decided I should probably go to A&E. Once again, not wanting to inconvenience the emergency services for their free transport we decided to take a taxi. A taxi to the hospital after getting hit by a taxi. The irony! The modern-day equivalent of ordering a steak pie from Mrs Lovett moments after getting decapitated by Sweeney Todd. Needless to say, I chose their rival taxi company who offered a far more luxurious service which kindly didn't involve kneecapping me on arrival.

Arriving no more unscathed than I had set off, I limped into A&E at Edinburgh's Royal Infirmary and was immediately greeted by paperwork and scenes of carnage. Having maintained minimal skill from *El Nombre* (Did I mention this guy in the first book? If not, then I can only apologise for such a glaring childhood omission. For anyone unlucky enough not to experience *El Nombre*, he was some sort of mysterious Mexican street rat guy. He wore a sombrero and swung in on a rope to teach the townspeople how to draw a number correctly because the narrative leaned heavily towards the assumption that they were too thin in the brain department to work it out for themselves. Regardless of him floating perilously close to the glass ceiling at the top the cocky fictional rat scale, my primary two class at West Linton Primary adored him. You know how *Borat* was frowned on heavily by the people of Kazakhstan because it was a bit culturally insensitive? Well, the good people of Mexico must have been furious with this little sombrero-wearing rodent in the '90s. I have no doubt they would have called Ofcom to complain about him if it weren't for the fact according to *El Nombre*, none of them owned a telephone on account of their lack of number awareness.) That bracket was far bigger than initially intended, so I feel obliged to restart the previous sentence again so you don't have to pilgrimage back to the start. Having maintained minimal skill from *El Nombre* or joining my letters at primary school, My handwriting was experimental at the best of times, but it was an uphill battle trying to fill out a form with wrists that by this point had begun to resemble the wobbly men behind goals at football stadiums. I can only assume Sara helped me complete the form, otherwise It would have read something like:

Name of Patient: ~~c~~r~ ~o~~.

Date of Birth: 1~ 0~ 19~~.

I had to wait around two hours to be seen because it appeared I rather unfortunately mistimed my visit and it coincided with national stab someone day. To be clear, the stab victims I encountered all seemed high as kites and in non-life-threatening situations.

One particularly charming gentleman had a party trick which involved spraying blood from his neck over one of the nurses, so it's probably OK that I'm being so nonchalant about their unfortunate predicaments. I got x-rayed and all that then I left with two wrist fractures and a bandage for my knee to help the swelling go down. I was in pain from naively turning down their kind offer of co-codamol, but quietly relieved that I hadn't wasted their time and there was a legitimate reason for me being there. I'd love to tell you that in an act of defiance we walked six miles back to Leith in the early hours of the morning, but no, we took another bloody taxi.

I tried to go back to work the following week largely because I always felt guilty about having sick days. Equally, I was a bit embarrassed about the whole event and wanted to get the inevitable "Taxi for Cobb!" jokes out the way. It turned out that not being able to type was a bit of a dealbreaker in a job which mostly centred around a computer, so I went home. Later that day I got signed off work for a month or so until the lion's share of the pain subsided. It took roughly six to eight weeks to heal, in which time Sara and my flatmates were a massive help as I struggled to open doors, hold a cup and even wipe my arse for the first few weeks (to be clear, I did wipe my own arse, but it required Jenga-like precision to avoid intense pain. Not sure you needed that level of detail but hopefully it adequately set the scene and hasn't put you off Jenga for life). What I hadn't anticipated was the time it would take to heal my brain's insistence of reminding me every few seconds that things could have been a lot worse. I was a nervous wreck being anywhere near traffic for a good while after it, and I'd wince any time I encountered a zebra crossing. Even nowadays, I'm still not entirely comfortable with them, but I've come round to the idea that it was just a freak accident and statistically I'd have to be really unlucky for it to happen again...

For the record, as of July 26th 2020, I haven't been pulverised on a zebra crossing again, I just felt the ellipsis would build up the tension.

Aside from the pressures of the job itself, I've got some fond memories of my time and the people I met over the three and a half years I worked there. I've lost touch with all but a few of them, but the individuals I worked alongside from different walks of life were really genuine and some of the nights out (aside from THAT one) were great fun.

At least that's what I tell people on my LinkedIn.

Pigs:

I saw an advert one day about someone regretting one day telling people they like Trolls because suddenly their house was overrun with the hair-raised hell-raisers. Trolls everywhere because people mistook a fondness for an infatuation. It reminded me of my grandpa Paterson, though in his case it wasn't Trolls, it was pigs. I'm not sure what it was about them, but my grandpa adored pigs and couldn't speak highly enough of them. I can't recall how it all started. Perhaps he casually mentioned it in passing on one of our memorable family trips to Gorgie Farm in the '90s and from there it stuck.

Each birthday or Christmas he would be rewarded with a bonus present from a member of the family and invariably it would be pig-themed. To begin with, it was a fairly controlled collection, a figurine here or there which would be placed on the mantlepiece or on the windowsill of their Edinburgh flat. Things quickly spiralled more than a pig's tail from there though. What began as birthday and Christmas gifts quickly morphed into basically any time we saw something pig-related, it would be snapped up and sent his way. Cufflinks, glass ornaments and board games were just some of the investments we showered my grandpa with for over a decade or so. At one stage, my dear grandma had to intervene as the pigs were hogging (pun intended) the limelight which had once been occupied by her expensive porcelain ladies in a variety of posh dresses and hats. The pigs were taking over, and I for one was absolutely delighted about this and I sense so was grandpa, not that he'd make such an admission on front of my grandma of course. Perhaps sensing a terracotta army-Esque siege from the porcelain ladies, my grandpa had to acknowledge that the pig collection had reached capacity and we should probably cut back on the pig paraphernalia.

The family mostly obliged, but when in 1997 my grandma and grandpa moved down to Peebles in the Scottish Borders with a sizeable back garden, pig-gate was bacon, sorry, back on- and this time there was a plan to get him a real-life pig for the garden. Looking back I'm pretty sure this was a well-executed exaggeration from my mum, but at the time my sisters and I were bouncing off the walls at the prospect of getting him a pig and naming it Charlie after my grandpa.

Sadly, Charlie the pig didn't materialise, but I always enjoyed the idea of turning up one day with a pig just to see the contrast of emotions between my unsuspecting grandparents.

In October 2014, I visited Amsterdam with Sara and we were passing a shop with a rack of postcards out the front. Sara absolutely loves a postcard shop. I, on the other hand, have a fairly poor opinion on everything they stand for.

I haven't sent a postcard since I was about ten years old because I was saddened to go the length of the summer holidays without having received one from my friends. Every day the postman arrived I'd enthusiastically leg it to the door to see if there was anything for me and every day I'd sulk back to the living room empty-handed. Unless I did the decent thing and collected the rest of the post that was lying there, but I was quite lazy as a youngster, so this was probably a rare occurrence. A few days before returning to school, my sister Gemma shouted that there was a postcard at the door for me. AT LAST! I raced down the stairs to find one with perforated edges straight out of *Smash Hits* magazine with a thoughtful, oddly articulate and well-written message from one of my friends on it. I was slightly suspicious why they were sending me a postcard from their holidays with no destination on the front; instead, it was a picture of The Backstreet Boys. Still, it was a nice message. My forensics weren't done for the day though. I further inspected this card which smelt curiously of fresh ink and found no sign of a stamp on it. It didn't take a genius to figure out Gemma had written a postcard to me in an attempt to lift me from my pit of self-pity.

On reflection, it was such a heartfelt sibling thing to do, but at the time, I felt even more dejected at the forgery and aghast that such a trick could be played on me.

So anyway, Sara was leafing through the postcard rack, and I zoomed in on one which had a pencil drawing of a pig on it. Much like seeing the Trolls advert, I instantly thought of my grandpa and his pig collection. Wasting little time, I purchased the pig card. I've never really been any good at writing postcards since being scarred by them at the age of ten, so I planned to keep hold of it and hand it to him when we returned to Scotland and I visited him for a cup of tea and a chat about all things Scottish football. I couldn't wait to see the glow in his eyes when I showed him the postcard of the pig, and it would throw up lots of memories from the family buying him an outrageous amount of pig-themed stuff in the past.

Sadly, I never did manage to hand the postcard over, my beloved grandpa tragically passed away the following month with very little warning. I'm sad and slightly remorseful that I couldn't get the card to him, but I'm happy that I can fondly look back on him and his fascinating collection. On the face of it, the pig collection could have been perceived as a bit random to those blissfully unaware of the circumstances. But to those of us that were in the know, each pig had a story behind it and each purchase was one of love and fondness for my grandpa and his wonderful appreciation for the animal. The fact the collection got so vast was no doubt in part down to my grandpa's kind heart that he couldn't bring himself to tell people sooner that the collection was getting out of hand.

I'm glad it went on for so long though as it's remained etched in my memory ever since and I think about him and the happiness he brought everyone he met any time I see something pig-themed.

Alongside some of his pig regalia, I was gifted my grandpa's old car, a silver Ford Fiesta from 2002. Sara and I had countless great adventures in Winston the car, including several miracle MOT passes which added to its folklore. I was extremely attached to the car and felt a sense of honour and responsibility every time I drove it. It can be hard being so emotionally attached to items which once belonged to family members though, particularly the larger and more sentimental the item. Sooner or later it can get to the stage where the sense of joy it brings can start to feel more of a burden to hold on to it. My grandpa wouldn't have wanted me to overthink it and get emotional about it, so when the opportunity came up to pass the car on to my cousin Scott in October 2020, it made perfect sense. Having not driven the car for eight or nine months I was pleased it could be put to use again and relieved that I no longer had to tie myself in knots trying to figure out what to do with it.

Winston and I sabotage a work photoshoot. Edinburgh, 2019.

I've always seen huge sentimental value in material objects that I closely associate with loved ones. Take for instance a shirt at the back of my cupboard. I might not have worn it in five years, but because I got it as a present from my parents one year, I feel an emotional attachment to it and don't feel ready to part ways with it.

The same went for the car. You might think it was just a piece of metal with wheels, and in a sense, you're not wrong. For me though, it was what the car represented that I struggled to let go of. I worried that by getting rid of it I was parting ways with my final memory of my grandpa. I needn't have worried as this, of course, wasn't the case. I'm slowly learning that we don't need objects to constantly remind us of the past. Sometimes all it takes is the sight of a muddy pig in a field, a rainbow above Tynecastle, or a chapter in a book for the happy memories to flood back.

Rock Star Pt III:

Once I'd arrived at the peak and planted the flag on my 20s, all of a sudden it was time to begin the onerous climb down to the big 3-0. It was becoming all too obvious that my dreams of being a rock star in a band were rapidly diminishing. The odds of carving out a path of success in music over the age of 25 felt extremely slim. It didn't help that *The X-Factor* had to introduce a pensioners category for the over 25s like they needed some kind of special dispensation. I remember tuning in to the first series back in 2004 as a moody 16-year-old when 35-year-old Steve Brookstein won the competition, and I thought 'Fuck me, who invited their pissed uncle? What's he going to sing, Sinatra?!'

The real problem I was faced with was less about my age, and more that I hadn't written a new song in about five years and I made little effort to get a band together so of course I was going to be up against it.

With opportunities seemingly few and far between, I jumped at the chance when one of my flatmates at the time was looking for a bass player to join the band he played drums in.

I didn't know the first thing about bass guitar, and I'd never really fancied it, but when the opportunity arose I couldn't turn it down. I booked a fortnight off from work and bought an Epiphone Thunderbird bass and spent all day every day of my holiday locked in my room learning how to play the thing. Resurfacing a fortnight later like a bewildered Chilean miner I still wasn't all that good, but I knew enough to cautiously navigate my new murder weapon. Plus, if I'd learnt anything from battle of the bands competitions at high school, if I at least looked like I knew what I was doing, I could probably blag it. Worst case I could always just turn down the bass amp and hope that both band and audience were none the wiser.

After a few practices, we played a gig to around 100 people at Electric Circus round the back of Waverley Station. Aside from head-butting an overhead speaker I'd miraculously made it through that first gig unscathed and watching the recording back the whole band played well.

That was to be my only gig with the band as they rejigged their sound a little after that night (which is a polite way of saying their manager felt a bassist was surplus to requirements and a laptop would do a better job). I wasn't too disheartened though; it was nice to have had that opportunity to play in front of that many people who were transfixed on the stage. I'd been accustomed to playing acoustic gigs for years to five or ten in a crowd who more often than not were only there out of sympathy, so to have a fully engaged audience was something of a novelty.

The DMS gig. Electric Circus, Edinburgh, 2014. (Credit: Alan Swan.)

As luck would have it, my friend Alex who was a singer/songwriter in a local band called Quiet as a Mouse was in attendance that night at Electric Circus. A few months later he asked if I wanted to join the band as their bass player had left.

I was slightly awestruck, and it felt like a dream being asked to join one of my favourite bands. Before that I'd been a regular at most of their gigs in Edinburgh and Glasgow as a fan before gravitating to selling tickets and t-shirts for them while they were on stage.

The first few weeks of rehearsals I felt an extreme case of impostor syndrome and it didn't feel real. It took a few sessions to come round to the mindset that I wasn't playing covers, I was actually part of the band.

After a little while, I got into the swing of things and put less pressure on myself, instead I channelled my energy into just enjoying playing in a band. I was finally doing what I'd longed to do for the best part of twenty years since I'd first heard Elvis Presley and Oasis and since I started designing tape covers for Euan and I's fictional band The Moonshakers in primary school. Alex and I shared a clear vision and determination for the band to succeed. In order to give us the best chance to do so, it was important to go straight to the recording studio to record an EP.

We booked into a high-end Glasgow studio called Ca Va Sound which had previously recorded blockbuster names like The Red Hot Chili Peppers, Paolo Nutini, Texas, and the queen of music, Avril Lavigne. We spent a weekend (and a shitload of money) recording two tracks, 'Snowflake' and 'Letter in my

Pocket.' While the costs were eye-watering to say the least, we were all in agreement that the songs merited it and the better the sound quality, the more chance we'd have pitching to management, record labels and radio.

I'd planned to sing backing vocals on both tracks, but that idea was cannonballed when I decided to channel my inner Paolo Nutini and stay up drinking the night before recording commenced. Day one I struggled to hold my guitar, let alone hold a note. Listening back to the songs I'm stunned my suffering isn't more apparent on the bass lines recorded that day.

If memory serves, I think we recorded those songs live as a band rather than slicing together our individual parts as it afforded us more time to get the tracks mixed there and then without needing to shell out another £500 for an extra day. Then again, I can't say I retained much from the first day of recording other than getting embroiled in a heated discussion about Scottish independence with our guitarist so, to be honest, I've got no idea what went on in that recording room.

(L-R) Graham, Alex and a hungover mess. Ca Va Sound, Glasgow, 2015.

Day two was mostly vocals, overdubbing and adding layering to the tracks from the previous day. With my harmonies still sounding like Dot Cotton from *East-Enders*, I wasn't involved in much that day other than drinking copious amount of coffee and passing judgement on what the rest of the band had recorded.

Sitting with Alex and the producer listening to 'Snowflake' in its entirety through the studio speakers at the end of that day was spellbinding and quite a triumphant experience. The song was swirling around my head on the train back to Edinburgh that night. I was convinced it was the breakthrough that would get us to the next level, and I could envisage the energy and euphoria of playing it live in front of a crowd for the first time.

A few months later we released the two tracks alongside a further two from the band's archive they'd recorded a few years before and titled the EP 'Memorybox' after the final track on the EP. It was a really solid recording and one I was incredibly proud of and could actually listen back to. My solo recordings which had gone before didn't have the same effect. I was quite embarrassed listening back to them. Perhaps as they were so raw, and it was inescapable for the duration that it was just myself and a guitar. The singer/songwriter genre wasn't something I'd ordinarily listen to or expect anyone else to, but I was now playing something I actually liked which was a bonus.

We were played on local radio a couple of times, but it was generally hard to come by, and the response was quite underwhelming. It was challenging work getting any recognition in the UK, but weirdly we were picked up by two publications overseas. The first one was a small blog in the United States who reviewed in between throwing out a recipe on how to make a homemade pizza. I got the impression that guy smoked a lot of drugs and operated the website from his parents' basement. The other was a Mexican music magazine who I can only assume mistook us for a bigger band as they gave us a one-page interview in Spanish. I retained barely any of my high school Intermediate B Spanish, so I relied heavily on Google translate to figure out their questions. Responding in English, Alex and I went into meticulous detail about our recording process and the influences behind the band. The magazine published none of that of course and instead ran with a question I firmly treated as a piss-take asking us who our favourite fictional mouse was. After calling Mickey Mouse arrogant and up his own arse, I regrettably decided to sum up British culture by referencing people's morbid fascination with Nando's and Selfie-sticks. Follow-up questions included asking us if we liked The Smiths, which of course we did, but they'd been split-up for around thirty years at that point so I didn't see the relevance in their question. They then went on to ask if we'd seen the recent Kurt Cobain film. My extensive answer to that one was "Ci." In their final act of valiance, the magazine managed to crop out our drummer Graham and guitarist Ali from the press shot and included one of Alex and myself looking forlorn and an unfortunate cross between Pet Shop Boys and Bros. Unsurprisingly we didn't ship out many t-shirts or CDs to Mexico off the back of that.

Alex and I, Bros 2.0.

The live shows with the band were great fun, and I particularly enjoyed moodily drinking red wine on stage and maintaining an un-arsed expression for the majority of the set. Choosing walk-on music was another highlight. The rest of the band weren't overly bothered by that sort of thing, but for me I saw the value of pumping the crowd up with some obscure music. Hot Chocolate 'You Sexy Thing', Will Smith 'Miami' and Toto 'Hold the Line' were my favoured go-to songs. Actually, I cut Toto out of the playlist after someone came up to me after a gig once and gave a glowing review of 'Hold the Line' with minimal reference to the performance that followed it.

In August 2015, we were about to play our biggest

headline gig to date at the Edinburgh's 300 capacity Caves on the Cowgate, right across from Bannerman's the venue I played my first gig in the city eight or so years before. The Caves was one of the venues I had always wanted to play, and I had every faith that we'd be able to justify playing there with a decent turnout. We'd managed to get the manager of a one-time hugely successful band to come down to watch us that night too, so everything was looking promising.

The evening was probably more stressful than it needed to be as the support bands hadn't shifted as many tickets as they'd promised and the singer from one of the bands who were about to leave before we'd even played had demanded cash for the four tickets they'd sold. After politely telling him to go fuck himself and his twee band, the familiar sound of Rod Stewart's 'Da Ya Think I'm Sexy?' sounded and it was time to hit the stage. I was angry at the support band but otherwise in top form as I couldn't believe I'd managed to twist the rest of the band's collective arms to agree to us walking on to King Rod.

The photos from The Caves were a bit shite, so here's one from Electric Circus in 2015 instead. (L-R) Ali, Alex, me. (Credit: Asitis.)

The acoustics were surprisingly awful and I couldn't hear my bass but I felt like we'd played a blinder at that gig in front of a respectable eighty people. I slightly seized up when I clocked the manager that had come down to watch us three songs from the end, but it was a strong performance regardless of the end of set nerves.

I emailed the manager afterwards, and he questioned why we'd booked the gig if we knew we couldn't fill it, adding that it didn't look the best that the venue was a little over a quarter full. I politely disagreed and pointed out that for the band it was more important that we aim high rather than playing it safe and always playing the same two venues in the town. Of course we didn't think we could sell the place out, but it was a thrill trying our best to. There was no harm in trying and failing, and it was one off the bucket list to play that venue. We managed to break-even and sold a fair bit of merch on the night too, so in our eyes it was far from a failed experiment.

The brief email exchange with the manager provided some valuable and eye-opening insight into the high expectations of the music business though, so it was clear we were up against it.

Outside of Edinburgh where we'd typically get fifty or sixty at a weekend gig, the other cities, for the most part, were half-empty. I had no qualms playing to low numbers, but it was a demoralising pattern going through to Glasgow to play in front of ten people and then spending money to travel down to London a few times a year to play to half that number.

Performing to low numbers, not landing any festival slots after emailing about 100 bookers/promoters, and the EP not getting the credit or airplay I felt it truly deserved made things quite difficult to feel optimistic about the band. To make matters worse, Sara had decided to go travelling and moved to Sydney not long after our Caves gig in August 2015. Sensing Quiet as a Mouse were my last real chance at being in a successful band and realising my lifelong dreams of being a rock star, I made the heart-wrenching decision to stay in Edinburgh to pour everything into the band. It wasn't going to be an easy year apart from each other, but Sara and I were both determined and incredibly passionate about what we wanted to do and equally as supportive of each other's choices that it made sense for both of us.

Australia Pt I:

Reunited. Sydney, February 2016.

Melbourne:

In February 2016 I flew out to spend three weeks with Sara in Australia where we would spend roughly a week in Sydney before embarking on a couple of city trips around Australia. On our travels, Sara and I took in Brisbane, Melbourne, and Tasmania. Melbourne had proven to be an absolute nightmare as far as booking accommodation was concerned. Everything was fully booked.

After a toss-up between a hostel straight out of a *Neighbours* murder special or an Airbnb down near the beach town of St Kilda, we opted for the latter which in our eyes was the least short of the two short straws. It was the one with the slightly less than 100% chance of getting chainsaw massacred. I wasn't overly enthused at the concept of staying in a house with another couple, but I was just thankful we had anywhere at all so I would just have to grin and bear it. With any luck, due to our busy schedule we'd be ships passing in the night anyway, so the chances of much awkward conversing would be minimal.

The decision was rubber-stamped based on the house photos, including a sweet and well-mannered looking sausage dog. A sausage dog that turned out to be a total dickhead by the way and nothing like the smiling, carefree all-round good guy that its picture suggested. I wonder if anyone else has ever been so clearly catfished by a dog on Airbnb? If you're not familiar with the concept of Airbnb, it's essentially folk renting out their house, or in this case spare room, much like your conventional bed and breakfast, but with fewer instructions and a Battleship like approach to a toilet timetable.

On arrival, the frosted glass bedroom and bathroom door combo was a bit weird. I'm not overly comfortable having to limbo myself out of view from the glass door facing directly into the living room/kitchen just to piss in peace. After nearly pulling a hamstring trying to yoga manoeuvre myself over the bowl I binned that idea and instead chose the easier route of sticking to off-peak times for my infrequent toilet trips of shame.

Shortly after the awkward welcome to the house hug we were instructed to "help yourself to anything you want" by the bubbly South American lady who greeted our arrival to her home. The dog clearly didn't inherit any of her manners or personality and barely bothered to make eye contact on our arrival. Some people need no further guidelines after a "help yourself" instruction and are quite happy to proceed to indeed help themselves to anything they want like it's an all-inclusive resort that they've splashed a few grand on, not someone else's house without a clear set of rules. Those people could be best described as brass-necked lunatics. I'm the sort of person that feels guilty asking for a water at a job interview even if my throat's dryer than the Sahara. By contrast, some members of society have no shame and can quite happily send the receptionist on a backbreaking mission round the corner to pick them up a lime Frappuccino and a cinnamon roll from Starbucks without so much as a second thought.

The first opportunity to test how much I was going to "help myself" arrived whilst making a coffee. Helping myself to a readily available stream of coffee? Sure, I can do that. Coffee's something that I would consider universally shared. So, when someone says "help yourself to anything you want" I'd be confident that the signs were all there to suggest the coffee was fair game and definitely an inclusion in the aforementioned "anything" category. The first hurdle arrived moments later in the form of milk. Was unopened milk included in the "anything" bracket? When presented with moral dilemmas like this I instantly revert to a worst-case scenario in my head out of reflex.

I envisaged the couple that owned the house and their demonic dachshund were all sat round their table later that night whilst Sara and I were out at a DIIV concert. They'd be debriefing and assessing how the first few hours with their new house guests had been. The trio would quickly reach the unanimous decision that we were terrible human beings on account of the fact that I broke the Airbnb rule of trust by breaking the seal of their previously unopened bottle of milk, rendering me an arsehole for life. On the other hand, if I went to the petrol station across the road to get our own milk would they take offence that I wasn't having any of theirs? I can safely say this wasn't a moral tug of war I ever envisaged having with myself.

I had to Google "Airbnb etiquette" before I was safe in the knowledge that I wasn't breaking any unwritten house rules by adding a mere shadow of milk to our coffees. Still, someone could have explained that to the bloody dog who from then on proceeded to treat us like a Guantanamo'd Margaret Thatcher as a result of milk-gate for the remainder of our stay.

Arriving back from the concert just shy of midnight we quietly let ourselves in the front door and were greeted by the dog who gave us a look as if to say, "oh it's you, ah yes, you pair look vaguely familiar, I remember you. Well, unfortunately you've caught me on a bad night and I'm going to have to pretend I've got no recollection of either of you. Now, if you'll excuse me, I'm going to scream the fucking house down so you get a shite review on Airbnb for being disruptive house guests." Then he broke into song.

That unfortunately wasn't to be the end of our nightmare. In fact, milk-gate hadn't even skimmed the surface.

The following night we went out to St Kilda Breakwater to see some penguins assembling by the rocks at sundown. It was easily one of the highlights of our Melbourne chapter, but the night started off rather unexpectedly. We went to a local bar for dinner which had a fish tank. There's nothing normally peculiar about a fish tank in a restaurant. However, on closer inspection of the tank, it was clear my eyes weren't deceiving me. There was a dildo stood triumphantly in the middle of the fish tank. Just plonked there, the fish brushing past it as though it were an innocent rock feature. It wasn't as though it was serving any great purpose either like it was a filter or a fish block disguised as a dildo (maybe that's how I started thinking about fish block golf balls?) it was just a regular no singing, no dancing dildo. Nothing else really happened here, and now I think about it, this particular encounter with the dildo in the fish tank wasn't exactly life-affirming or even worth writing about. In hindsight, this paragraph's probably a bit out of place. But not as out of place a dildo in a fish tank.

With the fish tank ordeal out the way, seeing the penguins clambering up the rocks later that evening was a surreal experience. To get so close to these little guys as they waddled along the boardwalk minding their own business was a real pinch yourself moment. I felt so lucky that we were able to experience that and it really hit home how once in a lifetime an opportunity like this was. We'd seen penguins kicking about in zoos before, but seeing them operating in their natural habitat was special. At one stage, I looked out across the moonlit water and saw one on the approach right next to where Sara and I were positioned. "Look, over there" I whispered to Sara so as not to scare it. We both watched in awe as it slowly made its way out of the water, then picked up pace and rapidly scurried along the boardwalk towards us at breakneck speed. It was then we slowly clocked that it wasn't a little penguin at all, it was a fucking massive water rat. "Fuck, go, go, go!"

Speaking of big rats, we arrived back at the Airbnb shortly after and were greeted by the usual rousing reception from the sour-faced hound once more. The couple were up and watching something and asked if Sara and I wanted to join them for a drink and to watch some Aussie TV. Unable to think on our feet we both muttered, "eh... yeah OK why not." What would follow was thirty minutes sitting rigid, fake laughing at a show called *Upper Middle Bogan.* Perhaps it was the situation or fear of upsetting their dog, but our conversation was minimal and thankfully they decided to call it a night after one painfully shite episode of something I've got no desire to put my eyes and ears through again. Once the episode finished the guy's laptop began playing music and he disappeared off to his room. Without warning, some pretty coherent sex noises started reverberating from his laptop speakers. Sara and I looked at each other with a look that said 'whatever that is we should definitely turn it off before they come back through and think we've put it on his laptop' and 'I bet it was him that put the dildo in the fish tank.' Scrambling around to switch it off without having a clue how to operate a MacBook, the guy appeared at the door and calmly switched it off for us without saying anything.

The final day we were up bright and early to visit Ramsay Street, the set of Aussie soap *Neighbours*. I'd grown up watching *Neighbours* and I adored everything about it. Some of my earliest memories involve tuning in with my mum at lunch in Fergusson View. She would watch from the sofa with a cup of tea or with some ironing, and I'd watch from my carefully positioned potty at the top of the stairs so I could combine two of my favourite pastimes. The promise of 365 days of sunshine, the odd death of a beloved character and a largely ineffective lothario doctor that was freely handing out prescriptions of his cock and balls to any woman that set foot in his surgery really painted a vivid image in my mind of the Australian dream.

There was a truly insufferable English guy on our bus on the way to Ramsay Street. He didn't hide his dislike of the show and his embarrassment of where his family were dragging him to. I wanted to turn around and tell him in no uncertain terms that this had the potential to be one of the best days of my life so he better keep quiet or get his act together otherwise I'd find Paul Robinson, borrow his wooden leg and skelp him over the head with it. Instead, I decided to tune out and rifle out loads of weird memories from the

TV show to the bus driver who seemed somewhat bemused and overwhelmed by my enthusiasm and attention to detail for obscure stories from the past that most other people had forgotten (sound familiar?).

Though ten times smaller than it appeared on TV, it was incredible to be standing on the famous street. Having the opportunity to visit the film-set where they had the pub, the café and the doctor surgery was a bonus, though the illusion was slightly shattered when I found out these places weren't located right next to each other and the actual folk from the show weren't casually stood outside their houses throwing boomerangs back and forth to one another as I'd assumed from an early age.

It's always special to visit somewhere that played such a big part in your childhood. The risk is that if it doesn't live up to the high expectations you'd built up in your mind over the years, it could taint the memories. This was far from a let-down and being able to walk around it and take pictures of every corner with Sara made it all the more memorable.

Sara and I at Ramsay Street. Melbourne, 2016.

The more sights we took in on our adventures, the more I realised how much Australia had shot up in my expectations in a short space of time. Sara and I were having the time of our lives out here and everything felt amazing. I started to question why I hadn't moved out the previous August with her and whilst we still had a few days left together before I had to fly home, I began dreading returning to Scotland.

Returning to the Airbnb of terror one final time we were a little worse for wear having slightly misjudged our bodyweight to beer ratio after the tour. Neither of us paid the dog any of the attention it had so badly craved and made a beeline straight to bed as we had a flight criminally early the following morning to the final leg of our whistle-stop tour of Australia.

Hobart:

We touched down in Hobart, Tasmania and as predicted in the forecast, once again I was rough as nails. I knew little about Tasmania other than the fact they spoke Swahili and the plains of the Serengeti were located there which was home to elephants, lions, leopards, buffalo, and rhinos. It turned out that was Tanzania, rendering my knowledge of Tasmania to a level which could best be described as marginally less than fuck all. The pilot must have got the memo about the fragility of my hangover that day because he slammed the aircraft onto the Tasmanian tarmac. Tumbling off the plane and trudging heavy-legged through to the baggage claim we were greeted with a scene straight out of those agonisingly trashy TV shows. You know the ones where a camera crew follow airport security around as they rugby tackle a pensioner or behead a child's teddy bear thinking they're smuggling a million pounds worth of crack only to find nothing but stuffing and an inconsolable child who had to watch their beloved bear bow out in the most inhumane way possible. The awaiting sniffer dog thankfully didn't pass judgement at the pungent stench of alcohol emanating from me and bounded straight towards a Chinese woman and a young child. Paying particular attention to the woman's bag, the dog was doing rapid figure of eights going absolutely apeshit over her backpack. If I had more faith that I could stomach food I'd have been right into the airport shop buying popcorn and sitting back to see how this was going to play out. With a look of fear and confusion, the woman had to slowly relinquish her bag much to the delight of the grass, I mean dog. Sensing we were blending in with the rest of the nosey bastards at the airport, Sara and I edged towards the tourist information leaflets to fake read whilst keeping an eye on the action to our right. Two policemen seized the bag and began to cautiously pull out contents. A few raincoats, a book, a flask and then the object of the dog's desires. A mango. They were smuggling a mango into Tasmania from Melbourne. Australian airports clearly stipulate that guns, explosive devices, drugs, sharp objects and mangos are strictly forbidden in luggage so they'd clearly just taken a big old shit on the legal system. The K9 exchanged glances with the criminals and glanced back at the policemen and raised both of its eyebrows as if to say "Well, well, well. Another day, another mango smuggler." I don't think dogs have functioning eyebrows, but if they did, that's exactly the sort of look the dog would have been giving. I was hoping they'd crack open the mango to find it loaded with diamonds and drugs, but rather disappointingly it looked just like your everyday run of the mill mango. Not long after the incident, I bought a mango and immediately smelt it. It didn't smell like any-thing, so how the dog managed to sniff that out from its raincoat cocoon I haven't got a clue. As for the criminals, their precious mango got launched in the bin and they were free to return to their life of casual fruit smuggling.

It's bad news when someone carrying a mango in their bag is the highlight of your visit to a place, but Hobart didn't really hold our interests quite like the cities which preceded it had. We went to see *Deadpool* at the cinema on the first night which we both felt reasonably guilty about. I feel like going to the cin-ema in a city you've just touched down in for the first time carries a pang of similar guilt to that of watch-ing TV when it's sunny outside. No matter how much you really can't be arsed to experience anything out-side there's still that age-old guilt that eats away at you for shunning the vitamin D and you can't fully enjoy the experience. Having said that, on this occa-sion, it wasn't sunny outside, it was pissing it down, and it had quickly become apparent that without a car there really was fuck all else on offer in Tasmania aside from *Deadpool*.

The first night we stayed in a pleasant enough hotel, but it was a little dated and quite out of the way so we decided our second and final night would be spent in a grander artsy hotel down by the waterside. Having checked in and dropped our bags on the second night, we made the most of our second day by visiting an old prison and then got well-oiled at a wine tasting. Now, I'm not exactly a sommelier, but I'm no stranger to a wine tasting. I feel like I've nailed the right level of faux-restraint and glass swirling to make it look like I'm not just there to get smashed cheap, then attempt to leave in a straight line with absolutely no intention of buying any of their expensive booze. I used to ridicule the couples on travel programme *A Place in the Sun* that would dupe the presenter and production company into thinking they wanted to relocate to Spain. They'd turn around at the end of the programme and wryly inform the host "D'you know what, Amanda Lamb? We've had a great few weeks drinking sangria and getting a tan which Channel 4 kindly paid for, but we're actually quite happy in our studio apartment in Birmingham thanks." The more I think about it, the more I realise I've been subconsciously adopting a similar shameless strategy at wine tastings with a straight face for years.

Leaving the wine tasting with a glow and a couple of folded up sheets of tasting notes that would never be looked at again, we returned to the hotel for a quick wine siesta. Wine siestas are widely known to be a woeful decision, but they just seem so tempting in the immediate aftermath of a liquid lunch. No sooner had we set foot into our room when we were greeted by a high-pitched fire alarm. Wearily making our way back out the way we'd just come in through the café, it appeared the front door had miraculously been taped off, and there were three fire engines and an array of police cars outside. I approached one of the waiters to get the lowdown on what had happened, half hoping if it were a real fire, it would burn my passport so my flight back would be delayed. "G'day mate (he categorically didn't say this, but I wanted to make it clear that he was Australian) we probably can't get back in for a while eh? It's a bomb alert." "Oh alright, cool cheers." I calmly replied. It was only when relaying his story back to Sara it clicked. A BOMB ALERT? A FUCKING BOMB ALERT? There was only one thing for it. We went to a whisky bar. As much as I wing it every Christmas, I'm not a whisky drinker. As chance would have it, neither was Sara and that became glaringly obvious by the second round. Overhearing the girl behind the bar was Scottish, Sara and I enthusiastically informed her that we too were Scottish. In our heads we expected her to greet us like old friends, maybe even crack out a glass bottle of Irn Bru that she'd been saving in case such a situation should ever arise, or at the very least like fellow bus drivers that wave and attempt to exchange smiles to one another when they pass by. In reality, she couldn't give a fuck. If anything she seemed angry that we'd outed ourselves as fellow Scots "Oh, I've not been back there in about twenty years," she flatly responded with all the animation of an ex-inmate reminiscing about their time spent in prison.

A little while later we rather impressively managed to navigate ourselves back to the hotel, which was situated a good 500 yards in a straight line away from the bar. It only took us about half an hour. Thankfully the bomb alert was a hoax so we could retire back to our still intact room. In further good news, we had the luxury of a sink each that we could throw up our concoction of bad choices into out of sight (but unfortunately still within earshot) of one another.

I woke up disgustingly early the following morning to listen to the second half of the Scottish Cup replay between Hearts and Hibs. Hearts got beat 1-0. How did I respond? I vomited in my allocated sink and went back to bed.

Flying Home:

After the Tasmania experience, Sara and I returned to Sydney for a quiet couple of days and then before we knew it the holiday was over and I had to fly back to Edinburgh. A tearful goodbye without knowing when we'd see each other again was followed by the savage twenty-four-hour flight back. I was sat next to a nice friendly older woman for the first leg of the journey to Abu Dhabi. She explained that she'd been over in Australia visiting her daughter. Sensing an opportunity to reciprocate the conversation, I told her all about the holiday and how Sara was staying in Sydney whereas I was going back to Edinburgh to divide up my time working full-time in a bank and playing in a band. It didn't sound nearly as glamorous when I said it out loud. She was patient and seemed genuinely interested in the story, even if I had basically subjected her to a *Forest Gump* style bus stop ramble without the luxury of a bus she could escape on. Aside from boring my neighbour to sleep and watching a ton of shite films that I'd never heard of I spent a good amount of time on the torturous journey weighing up my options and thinking whether or not it was viable to move out to join Sara. With my brain doing somersaults, I drifted off only to be gently awoken by an air hostess shortly afterwards. She was handing something out, so I blindly accepted. I wasn't hungry, and I had no idea what time it was or what she was giving me but accepted as it was free and it feels wrong turning down stuff that you've probably subconsciously funded in your £1500 return ticket. Holding my hand out, she placed a freezing cold choc ice on it. Don't get me wrong, on a warm day you can't go wrong with a nice refreshing choc ice, but there seems something deeply flawed with handing out a choc ice on an aeroplane in what I presumed given the impossibly black sky outside and the mood lighting on the plane was not an appropriate time to be dishing out ice creams. I like nothing more than receiving unexpected food parcels on an airline so I can stockpile a small tuck shop in the mesh netting on front of me to dine on as/when I feel like it, but you're not afforded the same luxury with a choc ice. You have to eat it there and then or risk causing an almighty mess. I looked around, and a good three-quarters of my fellow standard class passengers were asleep and like normal people not going to town on a frozen midnight feast. Not wishing to cause myself a further existential crisis I bit the bullet (or choc ice to be more accurate) and tried to go back to sleep with brain freeze. It didn't work, so I put the film *Legend* on instead about the rise and fall of the Kray twins. The nice old woman next to me successfully slept through the choc ice delivery but managed to awaken and fixate on my screen just as one of Tom Hardy's characters was viciously stabbing someone for what felt like an eternity. I say viciously stabbing, I've thankfully never witnessed a real-life stabbing, but I think it's safe to presume that most stabbings would fall under the vicious category. I can't imagine someone un-viciously stabbing somebody unless maybe it's an accidental stabbing. Just to be clear, given the lead up to this scene and the conviction with which he did it, this was definitely not an accidental stabbing. In the corner of my eye I could see the open-mouthed horror on her face but felt switching it off would make it too obvious that I knew she was staring at my screen so I just let it play out for another thirty stab-happy seconds until both the guy on the screen and my hopes of any future plane therapy sessions with my peeping neighbour were well and truly dead.

Australia Pt II:

When I got back to Edinburgh, I got a promotion at the bank, played another gig or two and recorded some new songs with the band at another studio through in Glasgow owned by the band Mogwai.

Slowly but surely, and whilst I maybe hadn't realised it at the time, my heart wasn't really in the band anymore. I felt quite deflated that our last EP hadn't really hit the mark as I thought it would and our gigs started to dry up with the crowds at our shows out-with Edinburgh never really picking up. For me, the most important aspect of being in a band was to play live as often as possible as I felt it was the most effect-ive way to gel as a band and to grow an audience. Alex far preferred the recording process, so it was quite hard to agree on the best way forward that would suit everyone. I found the last recording session, for the most part, a fairly unenjoyable experience. I didn't have the same buzz as I had with the first EP when hearing the songs played back at us through the speakers. There were definitely some aspects of the songs I loved, but to my ears, the recordings sounded a bit like a band tired.

A large part of this was probably down to feeling conflicted as I'd just come back from a life-changing trip to Australia and everything in Scotland seemed a bit dull and uninspiring in comparison. The image of the band which had previously been my focus and sole purpose for staying in Edinburgh was now being rapidly replaced with the notion that I shouldn't be here; I should be with Sara.

A few weeks later I'd applied and been granted a career break from work, so I booked a flight to return to Sydney and moved out by May with the intention of returning to Edinburgh three months later to resume my job and band duties.

One of the best photos I've ever taken, marred by a stranger's arsecrack. Sydney, 2016.

Before I knew it, I was firmly in Australia's clutches and I'd extend my time away to nearly seven months and not return to the bank or the band.

I was uncharacteristically un-apprehensive about the move which as you'll know by now goes very much against my grain. This was mainly because it was actually really easy and most people did the hard parts for me, which I'm not ashamed to say is a wonderful scenario. The travel company I purchased the flights with got me sorted with a tax code and a bank account, and Sara had been out there some nine months already which was a godsend. To be clear, not because she'd been at the other side of the world, that part didn't exactly spark joy. It was because she'd already laid the foundations for her life out there, so I was able to quietly tag along behind her like I used to do on the rare occasion we went clothes shopping together. In that time she'd managed to find a place to stay and made a close group of friends, so all I really had to do was focus on not milking the jetlag as much as I had in February.

We were staying in an apartment in Chippendale, a five or ten-minute walk from the city's Central Station, or equidistant the other way from Redfern. Bandit territory as my mum would fondly refer to it.

There was a 300-metre pedestrian tunnel in the lead up to Central Station which, until I moved to London, would regularly be one of the worst experiences of my adult life when attempting to wade through its oven-like temperatures at rush hour. I found the tunnel to be a good gauge of how quickly I settled into the city as, to begin with, it was something of a novelty. Its endless glistening tiles were densely populated with bustling scenes and aspiring musicians like some kind of creative inner-city channel tunnel filled with an array of people from all walks of life. Two weeks in I was sick to death of it and its arrogantly long neck.

Our original plan was to stay in Chippendale for a few weeks then find another flat we could both stay in. Luckily, Sara's flatmates Pete and Sandy were incredibly accommodating and let us stay where we were and slightly (massively) bend the rules of the lease agreement for the duration of our time there.

At this point, I would have liked to post a photo of the street, but unfortunately, the only picture I could find was this little number when we had the honour of being visited by the Australian Banksy one evening, or 'Wanksy' as one of my friends would so eloquently describe it.

'Wanksy.' Sydney, 2016.

The first few weeks mostly consisted of trying to get my bearings with long walks in the sun, then when I was sufficiently sunburnt and dehydrated, I'd head back to the flat to apply for jobs. Although I was still getting a little bit of money from the bank as per the rather generous terms of my career break, I needed a full-time job if I wanted to continue to fund my lavish sushi, iced coffee and Penguin Classics lifestyle. I had a clear idea in my head the sort of job I wanted; I wanted a bar job like that guy on the old Stella Artois adverts. I'd lounge about a pool all day then once every few hours someone glamorous would slow motion descend the staircase to my oceanside bar. I'd panic pour them a refreshing pint of Stella then get back to my slow jazz music and daydreaming. It took me to roughly page sixty-two of Indeed.com before realising that this dream was going to be hard to come by.

Whilst still in the honeymoon phase of blissful unemployment I'd get the train out most evenings to a place called Strathfield to meet Sara once she'd finished work. From there we'd travel back to the apartment together or go out for dinner. Sometimes I'd arrive early so I'd go and grab a coffee and sit in the tree-covered park in the square across from the station. It was in that park that I'd learn my first harsh lesson about the perils of Australia. People always warn you about the dangerous animals in Australia that will try to murder you the moment you step off the plane, i.e. spiders, snakes, crocodiles, and sharks. What they don't tell you about is the number of times you'll get shit on by low flying birds. A well-timed westerly wind narrowly diverted a bird shit to the mouth when I turned around to see if Sara had arrived at the station as a bird's black and white paint-ball collided against my cheek with marksman like precision. Like most people, I keep a mental note of the last time I've been defecated on in public by a bird, and that was the time I was when I was fifteen or sixteen and waiting on a bus to Edinburgh. I was doing my usual routine of trying to look cool in front of one of the many girls I didn't necessarily fancy at the time, but given any form of small talk, I would have gone into a full-blown high pitched meltdown. As the bus approached, a bird restyled my hair with the contents of its stomach. I tried frantically to get rid of it with my sleeve to no avail as I snuck past her on the bus with my freshly styled George Clooney hair.

Given my hit rate was now once every eleven or so years, I figured I'd be safe until my late-thirties. I wasn't. In the space of seven short months, I'd been targeted a further four times. Perhaps most unwelcome of all was the time at the races where I was giving a newly purchased light blue blazer its first run out. Maybe it was the good luck I needed that day as Sara and I won a fair wedge, but that money would quickly evaporate on a taxi home and a dry cleaning bill for my aforementioned shat on jacket. When I dropped the blazer off at the dry cleaners the following morning, the lady appeared concerned at the stain and quizzed me on its origins. After alerting her to the fact it was a bird's handiwork, she said it should be fine on one condition. "Do you know if it ate any berries?" she quizzed me from behind the desk whilst appearing to stare straight through my soul. I could file this question in with the ever-expanding folder of ones I don't know how to answer without sounding sarcastic. I confessed that I regrettably hadn't managed to get a proper look at the flying assassin so I couldn't be sure of the contents of its pre-match meal. I left it in her capable hands, and to my relief, it came back all clear a few days later.

So yeah as I was saying, I needed a job.

I found out one of the handful of agencies I'd applied to had secured me a role at a call centre in nearby Rhodes (Rhodes in Sydney, not Rhodes in Greece. Although given how long that bastard tunnel was at the train station the commuting time would probably be the same) which would be starting the following week. I was having birthday drinks with Sara at the Opera House when I found out, so we celebrated with more drinks before heading out to see Scottish comedian Daniel Sloss perform at the Enmore Theatre.

Before that though, I received another lovely surprise. As I sat swigging from a £10 bottle of Corona and looking out at the Harbour Bridge feeling blissfully content whilst the sun began to go down, a bird flew by and shat on my nice yellow shirt.

Lovely photo. Right before I was shat on. Sydney, 2016.

Australian Call Centre:

The job was in an outsourcing company for an initial four-week contract which eventually extended to a little over four months. To start with there were five or six of us working our way through an outbound dial-out system to update client addresses. This meant call after call of asking people to confirm or update their address. There was some sort of a target to aim for but each day was pot luck as to whether or not the customers you called believed you and gave you details or thought you were trying to scam them out of their life savings. Having worked at the bank for so long this kind of thing was a scenario I was all too familiar with.

I remember one landmark occasion when I was screamed at and told to "fuck off back to Japan" with my accent. I informed my faceless attacker that I'd never had the pleasure of visiting Japan, but I heard it was lovely and then she slammed the phone down.

To my knowledge, this was the first time someone

had been racially abusive towards me, albeit severely inaccurately and not in the way I was expecting. If she'd told me to fuck off back to Scotland I'd have gladly reassured her that she needn't worry as I was only here on a temporary visa, and if it put her flawed racist mind at ease, I was paying my fair share of taxes. On a serious note, a small throwaway comment launched at a point of frustration like that can have such a lasting impact on people's lives. I recognise I was fortunate to be born into a privileged position, one in which I had no control over and one where I'm seldom subjected to something like this. Others are born into a struggle where this kind of thing is a daily occurrence and the fact that in 2020 someone's place of origin or race can still be deemed in any way inferior by another saddens, angers and puzzles me.

Before long that work ran out, and three of us were moved next door to a similar role in a bigger project. I won't bore you with all of the details, but after a couple of months, I started assisting one of the managers with call listening and team meetings. This meant working separately from the rest of the team in a room overlooking the office. Our first manager was great and a real sweetheart with her team's best intentions at the heart of everything she did. When she went on to a new job, a replacement arrived for a couple of weeks. She was the polar opposite and went on a mad sacking spree, unlike anything I'd ever seen before. As you've discovered, the cinema wasn't averse to a sacking here or there, but this was two weeks of cold-blooded carnage. At one stage it felt like we were operating a one in, ten out policy, such was the haste of her evictions.

Sensing the mood was at an all-time low, I decided something had to be done to lift spirits or distract her from her reign of terror. When she popped out for lunch one day, I gave the apple on her desk a bit of a makeover. I transformed it into Kermit the Frog and paraded it around the office for validation before returning to my desk. Upon her return, I was sure she'd hit the roof, but to my surprise, she found it amusing and fully endorsed my actions. I think the fruit decorating began when I was in the canteen one day and noticed the stickers on the apples and bananas had given each one a name. From then on, I began to give each fruit their own identity because, in my head, it seemed like the obvious thing to do.

Now, I'm not going to pull out a line graph which demonstrates how the subtle act of decorating a piece of fruit attributed to the drastic improvement in morale and staff turnover, but what a bloody coincidence.

I'd follow-up the Kermit the Frog apple with a pear that looked like Shrek, a macadamia nut which somewhat offensively resembled one of the staff, an apple that doubled as one of the *Teenage Mutant Ninja Turtles* and perhaps my favourite of all, an apple modelled on Medusa complete with jelly snakes coming out of her eyes.

Sadly I wasn't joking.

After a few weeks, she left the company to start a new role which she informed me she was really excited about starting as her first assignment was to sack eighteen people.

Our remaining staff and the fruit bowl were fucking ecstatic when she left.

Road Tripping:

Four of our friends, Tim, Lucy, Matthew and Amber, came over from Scotland for a fortnight visit in July. Together the six of us embarked on a trip down Australia's east coast. Starting up at Airlie Beach just off Hamilton Island, in the space of ten days or so we took in the Whitsundays, Noosa Heads, Nimbin, Byron Bay and the Central Coast.

Whitsundays:

For the Whitsundays leg of the trip we booked in for a two-day boat trip out to the edge of the Great Barrier Reef. We would set sail around some of the seventy-four islands, snorkel, catch some rays, stop by a few beaches, drink all day, marvel at the stars, and just be at one with the ocean man. On paper, this seemed like it would be nothing short of paradise.

We flew into nearby Hamilton Island and arrived at

our hostel for the night in Airlie Beach. We rocked up nice and early so we could explore the place and have a quiet one ahead of the boat trip the following morning. Having quickly established that there was bugger all of any significance to amuse ourselves with in Airlie Beach other than copious amounts of alcohol at the hostel bar, the male contingent proceeded to get heroically drunk. The hostel bar had a karaoke night later that evening which I felt was a perfect opportunity to flex my vocal talents to the group and the rest of the bar. I sang 'Tribute' by Tenacious D so well that I thought they would award the act of the night bar tab to me straight away. I was so invested in the song that when I reached for the high note at the end, I went for a knee slide. A signature which I'd been perfecting since my open shirt Rod Stewart 'Da Ya Think I'm Sexy?' days. The unfortunate mistake I made on this occasion was I momentarily forgot that I was wearing shorts and performing on a stone floor, so my knee slide successfully cut open both of my knees. I finished the song in a small pool of my own blood which given the muted reaction I got suggested this wasn't really something the audience were after three songs into the night. Hoping to redeem myself, Tim, Matthew and I requested to perform Wham's 'Last Christmas', but the DJ allegedly didn't have the backing track, so instead we opted for a Ronan Keating megamix. To be clear, it wasn't meant to be a megamix, but Tim somehow managed to sing the wrong Ronan Keating song. Matthew and I were a delivering a slightly lacklustre in quality but no shortage of passion rendition of 'When You Say Nothing At All.' As is customary in a karaoke environment, the backing track was also playing the same song and the words on the screen were that of said song. Remarkably though, Tim managed to sing another Ronan Keating song, 'Rollercoaster' in its entirety word for word with impeccable timing which was some feat. Seemingly undeterred and none the wiser of his colossal mistake he said "Guys, I think one of you might have been singing the wrong song."

Unsurprisingly we didn't win the competition and as with any great night out, the evening ended in McDonald's having just received a lifetime ban from the Irish pub across the road. Much like the time I threw a shell in a swimming pool in West Linton, apparently it's equally frowned upon when you throw a plastic glass at an optic in Airlie Beach to try to get the attention of the bar staff.

Waking up bright and early the following morning we trudged down towards the boat armed with crates of beer and bags of wine that we'd bought the day before. (We ended up leaving the majority of it untouched on the boat given how much the night before had spiralled out of control.) It was decided that day one would be our allocated visit the beach and drink in the sun day and we'd leave the more strenuous water-based activities of snorkelling and canoeing to the following day when we were less bleary-eyed.

Day one passed by without much drama. We visited the picturesque Whitehaven Beach where they'd recently filmed one of the Pirates of the Caribbean films. It was one of the newer ones so everyone, including the director, had lost interest by that point. I quickly established that whilst it's nice being on a desert island surrounded by friends in the blistering heat there's a severe lack of things to amuse yourself with. Maybe I'd taken in too many breathtaking sights that year, but whilst the others caught some sleep on the beach I was bored and started digging holes trying to keep my beer cold which didn't work in the slightest.

(L-R) Amber, Sara, Lucy, Tim, me and Matt. Whitehaven Beach, 2016.

The second and final day we took to the water for a

spot of snorkelling around the coral reef. "Look guys, it's super important you respect the coral. It's dying so please, whatever you do don't touch it." Our boat captain warned us. What he failed to tell us was that in some cases the coral was at knee height, so it was extremely hard to avoid the stuff. As I plunged into the water I immediately booted a bit of coral, then again and again. After some panic floundering, I managed to swim towards the rest of the group and spent a couple of minutes bobbing about uncomfortably in the water before going underwater to investigate my surroundings. Time seemed to stand still as I marvelled at the wide-range of multi-coloured fish gliding past seemingly untroubled by our visit. It wasn't long before the clock started up again and I began frantically swivelling my head around like the girl in *The Exorcist* to make sure we weren't surrounded by any bloodthirsty sharks. By this point, my goggles had started filling with water which caused my contact lenses to feel like they were drowning in my eyes. With that predicament, I decided to call it quits and float back in the direction of the boat. They don't paint that kind of picture on the holiday adverts. They're rammed full of happy couples perfectly backflipping off the boats straight into Nemo's back garden where they see The Little Mermaid playing a coral xylophone and smiling sharks playing underwater frisbee with SpongeBob SquarePants. Not someone involuntarily becoming entangled in the sacred coral reef, getting a mask full of the sea, and blindly planning exit strategies from sharks.

Having had more than enough of the snorkelling, Sara and I boarded a canoe and went round in circles a few times before clambering back on the boat. With everyone safely back aboard, we sailed back towards Airlie Beach.

I've definitely made that boat trip sound a lot shiter than it actually was and in fairness other than when I was in the water, hungover and bored to tears on a beach, or trying to brush my teeth in a bathroom which had other people's shit floating about the floor on account of the toilet overflowing, I had a marvellous time.

Noosa Heads:

Flying into Brisbane, we hired a car which would be our transport for the rest of the trip. The white seven-seater Kia Carnival was a formidable sight.

Sia the Kia. (We listened to alot of Sia 'Cheap Thrills' in that car.)

Having never driven an automatic before I was now one of three drivers entrusted with transporting a seven-seater beast containing Sara and two other couples some 1000km back down the road to Sydney. It was a daunting prospect, but I had time to compose myself as Matt would be taking the reins first and I was in charge of the map so I could park my fears for another few days.

With Tim and Lucy spending the night at one of Tim's relatives in Brisbane before joining up with us the following day, the four of us set off for Noosa on Queensland's Sunshine Coast, two hours north of Brisbane. In the height of the Australian Summer from early December- late February, Noosa Heads is heaving, but it was something of a ghost town when we visited in July. As a result, a quiet night ensued which was just what the doctor ordered after the Whitsundays episode.

The following day we (Matt) drove to pick up Lucy and Tim and bring them back to our hostel in Noosa. For one reason or another, we set off early so we could visit a big pineapple beforehand. Having seemingly zoned out of the ins and outs of what it was and why we were going there I wrongly presumed it was a real-life pineapple in a field. It wasn't. It was an ageing plastic pineapple by the side of a road in the middle of nowhere. Inside it was a pineapple lover's dream with some history about the origins of the fruit, a few old tins caked in dust and no shortage of pictures of the exotic fruit in a variety of different poses. As if that wasn't enough, there was a lookout tower giving you picturesque panoramic views of the nearby motorway.

(L-R) Amber, Sara, me and Matt. The Big Pineapple, Queensland, 2016.

The unfiltered view from the Pineapple.

Nimbin:

Nimbin had a famously friendly laid back '60s vibe with a good majority of the village cheerfully off their tits on homemade drugs. It was basically Australia's answer to Woodstock or the Traquair Fair. Many viewed the place as a tranquil retreat where they made you feel instantly welcome in their peaceful village. Having once again failed to adequately research where it was we were going I was instantly on edge when I spotted a large group sporting tie-dyed t-shirts sat in a circle around a tepee in a field next to the hostel. As we unpacked the car, I could hear what sounded like monkeys in a nearby tree. I asked the receptionist whether or not there were actual monkeys in the trees, and she said "No, there's no monkeys here" before proceeding to burst out laughing for a solid un-exaggerated five minutes. So, we'd established that a) there were no monkeys and b) the receptionist was off her face. As she managed to contain herself long enough to direct us to our room, I pointed out that she forgot to give us any keys "Oh, we don't have any keys here. Everyone's really friendly." she reassured us. 'Fuck sake, we're all going to die.' my brain and mouth said quietly and simultaneously.

Traipsing through the ~~hippy commune~~ hostel to our room we passed the communal area with three housemates eating cereal in the dark transfixed on a documentary about gorillas on the *Discovery Channel*, making my job of throwing out borderline offensive stereotypes so much easier.

Maybe I've seen too many horror films where the well-mannered hippies turn into murderous psychopaths the minute it gets dark, but I was unwilling to let my guard down until we were safely back in the car the next day. It didn't help that when we made our way down the poorly lit and winding road to the village pub that night we spotted a suspicious-looking pair at the side of the road who we felt certain were either brother and sister, lovers, or both in animal onesies.

By some miracle, we all woke up alive the next day. I'd barely slept a wink that night through fear of getting an axe through the skull, but I was in a jovial mood having survived so once we'd packed the car at the crack of dawn, we set off for Byron Bay. I was on driving duties for the first time which I'd anticipated would cause me to be a bag of nerves, but given it meant I was in control of getting us out of the place I floored it down the hill. As we neared the bottom of the hill we passed the creepy brother/sister/lover onesie combo again who l was delighted to see disappear off into the distance of the wing mirror as I nervously glanced back to see if they were tailing us.

Byron Bay and the Central Coast seemed to pass by at the blink of an eye with surprisingly smooth driving and minimal drama. We went surfing in Byron Bay and had booked to go whale watching the following morning, but that got cancelled due to high winds so all in all it was a relatively quiet couple of days. A few days later our road trip was over and the guys were on a flight back to Edinburgh.

Whilst I was a self-confessed paranoid drama queen for a good chunk of that trip, it was a standout moment of our time in Australia as it took us to beautiful locations and further solidified a close bond between friends. It also made me realise that contrary to my previous beliefs, sharks, seven-seater cars, and a quiet village community who liked a bit of puff aren't all out to kill me. Well, apart from that onesie wearing incestual couple. They looked like they were definitely up for a bit of murder.

New Zealand:

In August that year, Sara and I flew out to New Zealand for a week's holiday/perfectly above-board way for Sara to renew her visa offshore before flying back to Sydney.

When I think of New Zealand I don't think of an unnecessary amount of sheep and hills, I think of Hobbits, Gandalf and pissed off dragons. I rarely planned an itinerary but, in the build-up to this trip, I was nose deep in a *Lord of the Rings* location book Katie and Jeff had lent us. The majority of key locations from the original films and the follow-up *Hobbit* trilogy were located in the South Island, but Matamata, where Hobbiton was situated, was luckily just a few hours drive away from where we were staying in Auckland so this was an absolute must-see.

After a brief tour of Auckland (God it's hilly. I know I've lived in Edinburgh for a good third of my life but Jesus Christ Auckland's next level and verging on inconsiderate) we booked tickets later that night for the Hobbiton tour and decided to rent a car for a few days rather than getting a bus there and back from the city. Our logic behind this was so we could find our own way there without any fellow unbearable *Lord of the Rings* geeks trying to get us to recite the names of all of Bilbo's troll mates or quiz us on which Orc we thought was the biggest wanker.

As soon as I clocked the meeting point and gift shop in Matamata, the fourteen years pent up excitement went to my head and I managed to pick the wrong lane and inadvertently drove the wrong way down a one-way slip road to enter the car park. It was no more than about a ten-metre stretch of road with no traffic coming the other way and an easy mistake to make as both were right next to each other without much divide. In my typically worried head, I was convinced I was going to end up on a feature in New Zealand Traffic Cops and get deported before I got to see Hobbiton. Sara being the rational one in our relationship managed to calm me down and we signed in at the gift shop. I spent a surprisingly restrained amount of money on *Lord of the Rings* merchandise (I bought four things but that's reserved isn't it?) and boarded the minibus which would take us to Hobbiton.

It's impossible to do the place justice, but I have no shame in saying it was easily one of the most memorable days of my life. I could quite easily live in a small hobbit hut with Sara and a vegetable patch and be happy for the rest of my life. Sadly, on the drive home I had to concede that this dream probably wasn't viable given the house height would cause us chronic back pain in later life and there was, of course, the very real possibility that I'd get sentenced to life in prison for my driving offences earlier that day and banished from Middle Earth for life. Still, what a great day!

Sara and I at Hobbiton. New Zealand, 2016.

Making full use of the two-day car rental, we decided to get back out on the road early the following morning and drive a couple of hours down to Waitomo to visit the world-famous glow-worm caves. I say world-famous, I'd never heard about them before, but I read that Katy Perry had visited them in 2011 so in my eyes that meant it was now firmly in the world-famous bracket.

Sara and I piled onto a small boat with about ten others and sailed into the middle of a black cave as the tour guide set the scene for what we were about to witness. I'm not going to underplay it, it was awe-inspiring. Truly a sight to behold all those millions of glow-worms clinging to the roof of the cave with their lights shining away like mobile phones at a stadium gig. The guide informed us that glow-worms lit up to attract passing insects which would become trapped in their sticky glow-sticks and eventually be eaten by the crafty glow-worm. Just as we began to think that these shiny cave dwellers were the most ingenious species around, the guide delivered a crushing blow. "The glow-worms eventually evolve into a butterfly with no mouth so they die after a day or two because they can't eat." Idiots. Their sole purpose in life is to ingest sufficient quantities of food so they can muster enough energy to bang each other in order to breed future mouthless butterflies. They're basically just shinier Lemmings. Don't get me wrong, the first two-thirds of their life cycle sounded terrific. If they're basically just eating and procreating all day no wonder they're glowing.

The initial plan was to head back to Auckland immediately after the caves, but after a quick scan of the map Sara suggested we pop by a kiwi park for a spot of culture to see some of New Zealand's national animal. I was fully on board with this idea, particularly as it didn't involve too much of a detour which was always welcome news.

Arriving at the kiwi park late afternoon it wasn't difficult to get parked because there was only about two other cars in the car park. Unsure if it was open, we gingerly entered the gift shop expecting the worst but were greeted by an enthusiastic woman who if you've seen *Tiger King* on Netflix was a ringer for Carole fucking Baskin. "Oh, HEY guys! Welcome to the Kiwi House, would you like to visit the park?" she asked. We nodded. Her breezy tone changed slightly when she had a quick glance at the CCTV and went "Oh umm.. it appears that all of our kiwis are asleep, but there are a few other animals in there or if you want I could go and wake one of them up for you?" Not wanting to cause a fuss or bother the snoozing kiwis we said we didn't mind and went in anyway to stretch our legs and have a look around. As we rounded the first corner of the park past a few lifeless kiwi enclosures the park tannoy announced that the eel feeding was just about to start. Sara and I stared at each other and we shared an expression which said, 'that sounds fucking awful'. We carried on walking around and aimlessly searching for signs of movement from anything which resembled a kiwi until we arrived at a big pond in the middle of the park. Once more we were steeped in guilt as we passed a staff member who was busy feeding the eels. She didn't have an audience, so it was just her and a small gathering of eels. Our agreed intention was to watch for a couple of minutes and move on, but before we knew it, Sara and I found ourselves leaning precariously over a pond feeding eels with a fork as they blindly swam up a ramp to munch on whatever it was we were plying them with. This routine went on for a good half an hour until the eel-keeper suggested we feed the eels by hand to which we unanimously declined. As the afternoon drew to a close, we didn't catch a glimpse of any of the main attraction, but we got to feed eels, and I can confidently conclude that was a once in a lifetime opportunity for us both.

Sara feeding eels.

With Sara's renewed visa through and my driving offences not flagging up on any airport computer, we flew back to Sydney a few days later. Picture Ben Affleck's white knuckle relief in the film *Argo* when his plane took off and in doing so he managed to evade the Iranian government, and you'll come close to the sheer elation I experienced when we made it out of New Zealand alive.

Celebrity Dogs:

For as long as I can remember Sara and I have shared a mutual love for celebrity dogs. (And a celebrity pig called Esther who the owners bought thinking she was a micro pig but she actually turned into a gigantic pig in what turned out to be one of the greatest stories ever told, but let's not go there.) I'm not sure which particular Instagram superstar sparked this off, it could have been Boo the Pomeranian (RIP) or Doug the Pug (Please don't ever die!) Whoever it was, we both became infatuated with them and their daily updates of being photogenic dogs thrust into the limelight. When Sara went to Australia and I was still in Edinburgh, I found out that one of the dogs we followed on social media (I'm already regretting writing this chapter.) was flying over from the US to appear at a local book shop to mark the launch of their owner's book about them. Two things crossed my mind when I got wind of the signing. First off, a twenty-seven year old man couldn't possibly turn up to an event like this on his own to meet Tuna the celebrity chihuahua/dachshund, no matter how famous the dog is. Secondly, I absolutely must meet this dog! With the positives outweighing the negatives, I turned up, queued for two hours and met the celebrity dog and got his "pawtograph" alongside two copies of his/his owner's book. The overpowering shame was eradicated later than evening when I got something like twelve likes for the photo I had taken with him on Facebook.

Tuna the dog and I. Edinburgh, 2016.

When we were both living in Sydney, after clicking on a photo of a pug dressed as a pumpkin or something equally engaging, I spotted an event on Nigella the Pug's Facebook page for her third birthday party. It would be a pug gathering in a park in nearby Surry Hills and everyone was welcome. It would have been rude not to go. Barely able to sleep a wink the night before I was buzzing for the big day. It's no secret that Sara and I are destined to get a pug one day. We've always had a place in our hearts for the wee squashed faced legends so we weren't going to pass up any opportunity for a bit of weekend pug-spotting. Not to belittle her achievements as a newly turned three year old pug, but with a rather modest sum of a hundred thousand Facebook followers compared to Doug the Pug's six million, Nigella wasn't exactly the Beyonce of the pug world, but she was still what fellow enthusiasts would class as a B-List celebrity dog. We arrived early incase it sold out (it was a big park so there was literally no chance of this happening). Upon entering the park the place was awash with pugs. Pugs galore. It was unorganised chaos with masses of grunting pugs going batshit crazy. It felt like we'd died and gone to pug heaven. Not ones to turn down the opportunity for a charity donation, we paid a few dollars to enter a pug play pen which people had brought their pugs along to with the money raised going to the local dog home. Sara got to hold a pug and aside from the time we went to Open'er Festival in Poland and she saw Dizzee Rascal, this was easily the happiest I'd ever seen her.

Sara and all of the pugs. Sydney, 2016.

At the end of the park was a tent which housed the headliner, Nigella the Pug. Her owner was perched outside the tent and warned us that Nigella was "quite tired and in a bit of a mood from all of the attention." Fearing another diva like the infamous Melbourne sausage dog, we went in and she had a party hat on and looked utterly miserable. Her brother Sterling, on the other hand, was the real star of the show and in his excitement managed to dive headfirst into a tablecloth, sending the table's contents crashing to the ground. They say never meet your dog heroes...but in fairness to Nigella, when I was three, I too would have likely been somewhat jaded if strangers had turned up to my party without any presents.

I'm not sure where I stand now with celebrity dogs. I fear they lead sad lives having been dressed up like Tudors and superheroes every day of their existence by their exploiting owners. On the other hand, they must get so many free combs and biscuits for advertising on social media, so maybe it evens itself out? Either way, I still probably follow more dogs on social media than actual humans and I'd jump at the chance to gatecrash another pug's birthday, famous or not, so who am I to discuss morals?

A Defining Moment
In An Otherwise
Pointless Chapter:

In late-September I left the call centre/fruit arts & crafts job at the end of my contract. I worked what little time I had left in Australia at a bank with stunning views overlooking the Sydney Opera House and Harbour Bridge. I had no idea what I was doing for the whole time I was there but I worked my balls off to act as though I did. This made me feel like an extra in *Neighbours* would if their only scene was to drink coffee from a cup which contained neither coffee nor liquid and they had to refilm the same scene fifty times a day over two months pretending it did. It had something to do with the Australian equivalent of a pension (known as a superannuation) and trying to get people to consolidate their multiple accounts into one account. I had about half an hour of training before I was launched in at the deep end which didn't bode well when I was in charge of someone's life savings. Anyway, ruining some poor pensioner's financial stability aside, I had a cracking view of the city and it paid well, so I was happy enough to ride it out. Nothing remotely interesting happened in this job aside from the fact I was sufficiently bored enough to spend my days staring out the window and daydreaming. It was on one of those days I decided to write an autobiography. Four years later here we are.

The office view. (Credit: Angus Marich.)

Farewell, Sydney:

To mark our final night in Sydney before heading back to Edinburgh we arranged to go with our friends to something called Dîner en Blanc. The idea behind it is that it's a massive party held in several locations across the globe and every year it's held in a new mystery location in each city. The night originated in Paris, which will become abundantly clear in a moment when you find out how utterly pretentious the whole thing is.

I was immediately sceptical of the concept as there were several rules attached. I don't think it's unreasonable to suggest that when you pay through the eyeballs for something with the word 'Dîner' in the title that you would expect them to provide dinner for you. Not in this case, you had to bring your own dinner along to their mystery location but if you wanted a drink with your meal you had to pre-order some of their extortionately priced wine. If that weren't enough, you even had to bring your own table, chairs and white tablecloth like some sort of posh T in the Park. Oh and the biggest rule of them all? You had to be without fail dressed head to toe in white.

As thousands of us congregated in Circular Quay (another place a bird had shat on me by the way if you were keeping count?) awaiting further instruction, I stood there cigar in hand decked out in my impossibly white jeans. Surveying the passing public who weren't part of this weird cult I tried to give them a look that said 'This wasn't my idea, I'm here against my will' and 'I know this looks bad, but I'm 60% sure that this isn't a Ku Klux Klan gathering.'

We had arranged to meet our friends in the square which perhaps wasn't all that well thought through when all you have to go on is "We're wearing white and we're in a square full of 2000 other people wearing white." It was like that really solid edition of *Where's Wally* when they're all decked out in red and white stripes. I bet this idea was deliberately ironic given the creator of this abomination, François Pasquier had apparently first thought of the concept back in 1988 when inviting friends to a dinner party with the request they all dress in white so it would be easier to find them. His friends could have done us all a favour and kindly told François to piss off and gone out for dinner without him in a restaurant they didn't have to bring their own plate to. Also, have you ever tried to eat anything whilst wearing a white garment before? It's the most stressful experience of your life, any enjoyment of the food is lost as the majority of the meal is spent on guard duty watching eagle-eyed for any rogue sauce landing on your immaculate white clothing.

Once we'd spotted the rest of our friends, we hopped on a boat which would take us to our mystery location. It didn't take long to realise that the event would be taking place on the nearby Cockatoo Island, the site of a former prison and where they filmed one of the Wolverine films that I hadn't seen, so I've no idea why I'm telling you this. As we neared the island, I started to feel relieved we brought our own food as given our appearance and apparent willingness to pay someone for a dinner we had to bring our own food to we were only one drugged up salmon fillet or asparagus stick away from a *Shutter Island* or Jonestown sequel. I stiffened up when I realised they could always just drug our wine.

At one stage during the meal, everyone was instructed to stand up in Mexican wave-like formation and wave their napkins in the air whilst some waved sparklers as an overhead drone took a photo of the scene. I've always been a bit hesitant about partaking in Mexican waves since my primary school music days when our music teacher went round the class and everyone had to play an instrument. This made for a very chaotic song which would have no doubt received a token rave review at the end regardless of musicality. It got three-quarters of the way round to me and I completely missed my cue to play the triangle. My unconscientious objecting derailed the whole performance like a solitary domino that forgot to fall backwards.

Despite hating absolutely everything about the theme and organisation, and the fact we were stuck on a prison island with no way off until the boat saved us, I had to admit it was a nice send-off to be together with all of our friends we'd met over there for one last time. We were lucky to have formed such a close bond with the group and there was definitely a lump in my throat at the thought of leaving them and a country which had made such a lasting impression on us behind.

Dîner en Blanc gang. Too many to mention.

The following afternoon we frantically tried to wolf down as many fine Australian delicacies like Darrell Lea liquorice, Shapes, Tim Tams, Doughnut Time, Pie Face and Zumbo macarons as we could stomach before boarding the plane. This was partly to experience the mouth-watering cuisine one final time and partly because I'd seriously misjudged how much we could eat on our final day so we had to panic shovel down as much as we could muster before we rolled ourselves through passport control.

Holding back tears for leaving and holding back vomit from binge eating, we passed through passport control and began the long journey back to Edinburgh and the next chapter of our lives.

Back In Scotland:

Within a matter of weeks of returning home, I was lucky enough to get a job in the Edinburgh office of the first company I'd worked for out in Sydney.

Sara and I were staying at our mums and dads houses for a few months while we got back on our feet and saved up a bit of money to move into a flat together in Edinburgh. This meant we were commuting back and forth to work at our respective jobs in Edinburgh. Sara travelled in by train each day from Berwick, and I drove in from Cardrona. Reverting to quiet country life after such an active time in Sydney took a bit of getting used to.

Cardrona made West Linton look like a hub of activity by comparison. It's a slower pace and there's no real drama in the village. Infact, there are only two occasions I can recall anything slightly contentious happening. First off during the village's annual Games Day, someone made some minor adjustments to the sign, and for a day or two, it simply read 'Gay Da' which I'm certain must have caused some blushes among the dog walkers. Another time l recall walking to the bus stop just as the heavens had opened and there was a mass frog orgy taking place in the middle of the road. I'd never witnessed anything like it, some three- and four-way action in what was becoming an ever-expanding amphibian swinger party. I was reluctant to stare that long, but I was also full of admiration for their mass public display of affection. I wondered if it had been pre-arranged hot spot or if it was just coincidental—either way it had to be applauded. When I returned later that evening, nothing could have prepared me for the scene of brutal devastation that lay before me. Most, if not all of the happy shaggers had been flattened by cars in what resembled a wet version of frog Pompeii. Some of them were still clearly going about their business at the point of their sudden and tragic demise. To this day it remains one of the most harrowing things I've ever seen, and I wouldn't be surprised if the pond census in the Scottish Borders took years to fully recover from the tragedy.

I liked the commute back and forth as in the mornings I'd set off just after 7 am so the roads were quiet. It reminded me of my dark commutes down the same road when I worked at the pub seven or eight years previously.

Aside from being away from Sara, I enjoyed the six months I spent in Cardrona as it gave me plenty of time to write, exercise and catch up with my mum and dad and our black labrador Bailey again after quite a bit of time away from them. Previously when I had returned home after dropping out of university, I was quite downbeat. I felt like I'd failed and had no back-up plan, but this time was very different. I had a job and everything was going great with Sara so there was a real positivity to my time spent at home and I knew it would only be a matter of time before I was back in Edinburgh.

That day arrived on June 10th 2017, when Sara and I moved into our first flat together in Leith. Well, sort of... that day had been marked off in the calendar as the day we were all set to move in, but I put a slight spanner in the works. Two days prior to moving day I'd managed to secure gold-dust tickets to Scotland v England in the World Cup Qualifiers. I far favoured club football over international football and that no doubt had a lot to do with Scotland consistently finding new ways not to qualify for major tournaments since 1998. I still feigned some interest every now and then, but it was becoming increasingly difficult to concern myself with the country's international footballing exploits. Scotland v England was another story. Perhaps I was exposed to *Braveheart* too young, or I was scarred from watching Gary McAllister's penalty miss at Euro 96, but I grew up with a competitive mindset that when it came to facing England regardless of which sport or what was at stake, we had to win at all costs. It could be lawn bowls, chess, or *University Challenge* for all I cared, I'd still be standing up in front of the TV praying for a Scotland victory whilst dishing out unpleasantries towards the Auld Enemy.

On a whim, I bought two tickets for £170 with the intention of surprising my dad with the tickets. My sister was up visiting my parents from London that weekend so that idea bit the dust very early on and that's when the guilt kicked in. I knew I probably shouldn't even entertain the idea of going to the game as it was a big deal moving in with Sara and we'd been waiting seven long months for that moment, but at the same time there was a persistent voice in the back of my mind that kept telling me 'But what if we win?' Unable to shake the unlikely possibility of a Scotland victory, I told Sara the predicament I'd landed myself in and went to the game with my friend David and it was decided we'd move in the following day instead. The guilt was at the forefront of my mind right up until kick-off when for ninety minutes, it was replaced with nerves and a proud sense of nationalism. Something not seen since I played the same fixture on *FIFA* in a pub against a stranger on my 22nd birthday. I scraped a win on penalties that night and showed no gamesmanship.

Scotland v England. Hampden Park, Glasgow, June 10th 2017.

Scotland routinely conceded in the seventieth minute and all looked lost until we won a free kick in the eighty-seventh minute. As Leigh Griffiths stepped up to take it, I had visions of the ball sailing into the back of the net to rampant scenes, but I held out no hope for this scenario to come to fruition. Seconds later, the unfathomable happened. He actually did it. The feeling was remarkably similar to that of scoring a late equaliser on *FIFA* against the English, but perhaps slightly more justified and met with more universal acclaim from others watching.

Having barely contained myself, I stopped goading the English fans for long enough to lift my head and see Leigh Griffiths lining up another free-kick from a similar distance. I turned round to David and went "Nah, surely not?" No sooner had I turned back to face the pitch when suddenly I was caught in a tsunami of jubilation unlike anything I could have imagined. He'd done it again and Scotland were 2-1 up with ninety minutes on the clock. Against the actual English! At Football! I cried, jumped to the heavens, fell down a bit, looked up to see if I could see Uri Geller hovering in a helicopter like he had at Euro 96 so I could flip the Vs at the spoon-bending weirdo. I dragged myself back to my feet just in time to see Scotland midfielder Stuart Armstrong gift wrap a pass straight to an England player. From there it found its way to Harry Kane who stabbed ~~me in the heart~~ the ball into the net to equalise for England with virtually the last kick of the game. I crashed back to Earth with a thump and felt numb, and also guilty as sin for changing moving day. If we'd won that day I could have almost justified it in my head, but a draw? To have been so close to a famous win was shattering and the draw felt every bit as bad as a loss.

I learnt two very important lessons that day. First off, don't scupper plans to move in with your dearly beloved at the last minute to go and watch a football match. Secondly, never ever invest your faith in the Tartan Army to grind out a result as they will always let you down.

Heart of Midlothian Pt II:

I remember it vividly, late one Tuesday evening in October 2017 news filtered through of the passing of Hearts' 1998 Scottish Cup-winning hero Stefano Salvatori at the terribly young age of forty-nine. Like many Hearts fans, I was shocked and deeply saddened. 2016 had been a 100mph conveyor belt of heroes disappearing off behind the curtain one last time, as a result, I felt somewhat worryingly desensitised to the whole thing by the end of that year. However, fast forward to earlier in 2017, when news broke of the untimely and tragic death of former Hearts player Stephane Paille on what was his 52nd birthday, this hit a little too close to home for me.

When you skid rapidly towards the ripe age of thirty, you begin to look regretfully down at the team sheet every other week before a match as you're sat there sinking your second soap-infested Tennents of the afternoon whilst failing miserably to flick all of the excess McCoys shrapnel off your shirt in the pub before the game; the whole time thinking 'When the f... did I become older than 81.8181818182% of the starting eleven?' whilst also questioning why on earth you even bothered to Google it. Even in 2016 when Ian Cathro began managing at Hearts, on several occasions I thought to myself 'Dear lord, I'm nearly as old as the manager!'

In the summer of 2017, I learnt that the only thing more depressing than that is when the heroes you cheered on each week as a bright-eyed, ever hopeful football fan die. The same players that you'd try to impersonate whilst kicking a ball about at school, the ones you'd pray for when buying a 30p pack of SPL stickers for your Panini album, and the same players you'd queue up for outside the players' lounge long after a game for a glimpse and an autograph, alongside your shivering, yet ever-present, old man beside you.

At the risk of sounding twice my age, there was something different and more honest about football-ers like Salvatori back in the mid to late '90s. The passion was real, the players gave their all for the jersey and for their adoring fans each week. There wasn't anywhere near the same level of media circus that surrounds even thr most mediocre of footballers today, many of whom are too consumed in coloured boots, sleeve tattoos, Instagram and Nando's to notice how lucky they are to do what they do each day.

Reading the tributes pouring in throughout that

week from fans of the midfielder's former clubs – Hearts, AC Milan, Parma and Fiorentina – it felt like re-discovering a box of childhood memories in the attic, as every emotion came flooding back, none more so than the first time I, and many Hearts fans, witnessed the club win a trophy.

Having just turned ten three days prior to the 16th of May 1998, even at that age I remember it feeling like a significant achievement beating Rangers for the club's first Scottish Cup since 1956. Although, looking back on the team Rangers had that day, including Brian Laudrup, Andy Goram, Lorenzo Amoruso, Rino Gattuso and Ally McCoist, it was some years later before it really hit home how much of a David and Goliath moment it really was that afternoon at Celtic Park. This reignited a fire and passion inside many Hearts fans who got to witness history thanks to the unscripted achievements of Salvatori and his teammates, putting to bed the horrible after-taste of 1986, which thanks to what I can only assume was careful planning from my parents, I managed to avoid.

It was about far more than just silverware that day, as any long-suffering football fan will tell you. The day your club wins a trophy, the things you remember and hold closest are who you shared the experience with, rather than the game itself. I was lucky enough to be at the game with my grandpas, my dad and my uncle and I'm eternally grateful to Salvatori and the rest of the team for forever engraving their name on that cup and in my memories.

The day following Salvatori's passing, like re-discovering that old box of childhood memories, I felt guilty that I'd inadvertently let what was arguably one of the best days of my life become little more than an after-thought as I'd been too wrapped up in recent times and I'd let what was by all accounts a disappointing past year at Hearts cloud my thoughts.

What really set me off, but filled me with immense pride of the Scottish game, was reading the reaction from fans of other clubs like Celtic, Hibs, Dunfermline and Rangers, to name just a few, who all offered their sincere condolences to Salvatori's friends and family upon hearing the sad news. It summed up for me what many people, myself included, can forget at times. Whilst it's often hard to see behind our masks, everyone's emotions and passions are the same when it comes to football.

Nowadays, Celtic are demolishing everyone domestically, and the predictability of it all can be tiresome and painful at times, but as I'm sure Salvatori taught the youngsters at his football academy in Brisbane that if you work hard enough, show enough passion, belief and desire as he and his teammates showed against a team that looked unbeatable in 1998, miracles can and do happen.

Thanks to Stefano and his teammates, I will always have treasured memories of that day.

◆ ◆ ◆

There's not much that can surpass seeing the team you've supported all your life lift a cup, and I've luckily managed to witness Hearts win the Scottish Cup on three occasions. The aforementioned '98 final, once on my eighteenth birthday of all days when Hearts toppled a Gretna side in a nail-biting penalty shoot-out on the 13th of May 2006, and more recently in 2012. When I say there's not much that can surpass seeing the team you've supported all your life lift a cup, there is one thing that can top it. Seeing the team you've supported all your life lift a cup after they've absolutely decapitated and publicly humiliated your bitter rivals 5-1 in one of the most one-sided games of football I've ever been on the right side of. On the 19th of May 2012, Hearts did just that, and it was every bit as magnificent as it sounds.

In the weeks leading up to the final there was excite-ment in the air for our date with destiny. Excitement which would promptly be replaced with intense fear when I realised what was at stake and the unthinkable repercussions should Hearts lose. Fast forward to the morning of the date with destiny. The family congregated at a bar on Bruntsfield Links to throw down a few early morning bacon rolls and some much-needed liquid confidence boosters. Not long after, our chariot awaited and we piled onto the bus in big numbers to begin our pilgrimage through to Glasgow for a liquid lunch in an Italian restaurant. Two corners into the journey, the bus broke down for what felt like hours, but in retrospect, it was probably only a mere fifteen minutes. Nonetheless, it wasn't a good start and there was a tense atmosphere on the bus for the remainder of the journey, desperately hoping that wasn't a precursor to what was to follow.

I realise now that I've made the mistake of trying to build tension when I've already given away the ending, so any picture of nerves I'm trying to gradually build here are in vain. So anyway, we went to the game and to partially quote the commentator from that day, Hearts were "rampant", and Hibs were utterly shite (the commentator didn't use that specific word to summarise Hibs' performance that day, but I'm sure he must have been thinking it). Goals from Darren Barr, Rudi Skacel (2), Danny Grainger, Ryan McGowan and some guy that played for Hibs made the final scoreline 5-1. The game was brilliant, the two-week-long bender afterwards was brilliant, and the bragging rights were brilliant. Best of all though, the weekend of jubilation with the family and the smiles all-round are something I'll never forget.

Dad and I at Hampden Park. Glasgow, May 19th 2012.

Watching Hibs suffer over the years has been a tremendous source of fun, and their misery and misfortune will continue to bring me great joy for many years to come. However, I'll whisper this next bit. When I recall my family and I's experiences of 19/05/12, part of me wonders how the green and white half of the city coped in the aftermath and if their fond memories of time spent with loved ones was obliterated by their team's epic capitulation that afternoon. It's hard to see past footballing rivalries, but when I consider the memories a cup win can bring, I would want everyone to experience that feeling at some stage in their life regardless of the colour of their scarf. I took off the maroon tinted spectacles for a split-second in 2016 after a few moments heavy recoiling that Hibs managed to finally lift the "big cup" for the first time in 114 years. I could see the tears and hear the relief and emotional release Hibs supporters felt upon hearing the full-time whistle, and it transported me back to my own emotions when Hearts lifted the trophy in 1998, 2006 and 2012. Don't get me wrong, I'm not delighted Hibs won the trophy by any stretch of the imagination, and I still feel a bit sick even writing this down, but to experience that unscripted and possibly once in a lifetime opportunity to celebrate with family is something I wouldn't want anyone starved of. For one day, and one day only, I was happy they had their moment. Actually, that's not entirely true. I was also happy the following day when they paraded the cup down a packed Leith Walk. Happy because by that point I was living in Sydney and no longer living on Leith Walk so I wasn't subjected to 200,000 people collectively helicoptering past my old flat whilst singing the bloody Proclaimers.

The Italy Trip:

This hasn't gone to plan. England got knocked out of the semi-final of the World Cup last night, finally putting the media's red and white throbbing confetti cannons down past half-mast and back into their box for another four years. Today should be a joyous occasion of getting pre-plane wankered, ironically blasting out Baddiel and Skinner's 'Three Lions' at every given opportunity without the fear of it actually "coming home" and flying out Italy to go and see Nick Cave & The Bad Seeds. That and hopefully building up enough courage to ask Sara to marry me.

I had it all meticulously planned out. My idea from the offset was to propose at the end of the book, but unfortunately, things didn't quite go to plan. I wasn't anywhere near finishing the thing. Infact, I was more behind than a primary school sack race and I didn't have anyone that would pick me up and carry me over the finish line on this one. Having been an eager Red Bulled up rabbit out of the traps when I started this project, I hadn't quite accounted for how emotionally grafting it would be. In a similar way to when a band on their fourth or fifth album revisit their debut which they may have been happy with at the time when comparing it to the modern-day, it can be more than a bit grimacing to look back at it through a microscope. Even with a year and a half of preparation, it won't come as a shock to most, but it's a lot of fucking hard work to get your ideas down and try to edit them, so they're legible to someone else.

Also, one Sunday morning, the usual routine of sitting in our alternating Hearts shorts watching *Sunday Brunch* with a bowl of coffee was going swimmingly well. That was until one of my favourite comedians Joel Dommett was interviewed about his new book which had a 'romantic twist' at the end. Hearing this immediately set off alarm bells. "Yeah, so at the end of the book I asked my girlfriend to marry me." He said, gleaming with joy. "Oh that's nice," Sara noted. "Ah yeah, that's nice isn't it?" I solemnly replied with the sort of false smile reserved for one of the other nominees that nobody remembers about at the Oscars. When what I really meant was "FUCK YOU JOEL DOMMETT YOU HILARIOUS BUT SELF-ISHLY ROMANTIC BASTARD." I really wanted to read his book too, but couldn't bring myself to do it before I finished this one in fear that I'd just make a less funny tribute act of the last chapter.

So that idea sank. Another plan I had was to play it a bit more low key and stream the video I'd made with a collage of photos of the two of us throughout the years through our TV. The video was soundtracked by The National's 'Dark Side of the Gym' (a song I'd try to unsubtly shoehorn into a first dance if Sara first agreed to the wedding and then to the song choice). It only took about three minutes for this idea to burst into flames. I uploaded the video privately onto YouTube and almost immediately received an email advising it has been taken down due to a complaint from the band's record label 4AD due to it being a breach of copyright. That was that beach ball punctured before I'd even set foot on the beach. If only this level of security had been about prior to the whole industry going tits up in the early 2000s, maybe bands wouldn't have to tour themselves into an early grave (or a late grave if you count the Rolling Stones).

Anyway, my timings were spot on in that video so my third and final plan would still involve the video, but I would propose to Sara in Italy. All I needed to do was buy a ring and ask her dad's permission.

Suffice to say, this didn't go well either.

The plan was bulletproof, I'd drive Sara down on Father's Day to her parents' house and ask her dad's permission during the football, he'd high-five me without taking his eyes off the game and I'd walk out with a spring in my step like some sort of overly chirpy '50s musical.

Much like South Korea, I bottled it during the first game, but I'd nail my tactics in the second game- no problem. It took me to the 80th minute of a tense encounter between Germany and Mexico to register a conversation on target with her dad. "Eh, David, well I er didn't think it would be this difficult." Informing my mum I'd missed my French exam because I was playing football instead fourteen years before felt like a breeze compared to this one. "So I was hoping that you'd be ok if I asked." He shot up from his seat and appeared in front of me, which was a good five steps away in one swift motion- I'm not even convinced his feet touched the floor until the emergency landing. Right on cue, Sara walks in. "Oh hi, I was just telling your dad that I hit the garage with my car again last week and wondered if he could come out and take a look at it." I served it up with about as much conviction as the "Hi mum and dad, I had a great night. No I've not been drinking. The diluted juice to water ratio was just significantly higher than usual that's all." from the high school days. No idea where that lifesaving ad-lib arrived from, but nonetheless it was accurate, apart from the fact her dad looked more uncomfortable than the German defence to my immediate right. Her dad and I marched eye-contactless, wading through the awkward tension to the front door as I struggled to negotiate my shoelaces, so I just tucked them into my shoes, paying little respect to the heels. Outside in the cold air, the words flowed a bit better. I explained that I felt bad (showing guilt is always a strong start) as his other daughter had only married two weeks before, but I'd been holding off for the best part of eighteen months since we got back from Australia as I didn't want to step on anyone's toes. He was fine with it, gave me his blessing and helped get the green paint grass stains out of the front of my car too, so all in all after a shaky start, it was fine. The adrenaline was still coursing through my veins alongside the overwhelming relief that I barely slept a wink that night.

The ring part was relatively stress-free. I did bog myself down with the usual price/metal/diamond stress that I'm sure everyone in the same position goes through, but other than that- I was happy enough with my choice.

Everything was in place, I just needed to get over the final hurdle. It turned out that would be one of the hardest parts.

Two nights before our trip, Sara found out her grandpa had taken Ill. Early the next morning, the day of the England semi-final v Croatia to be exact, Sara received a call and we rushed to the hospital at 4:30 am. After an extremely difficult day for everyone, we returned to Edinburgh, but Sara would need to return to the hospital the following morning with things looking increasingly bleak.

The trip would be put on ice, Sara stayed at home whilst I boarded the flight along with my parents. In the grand scheme of things, Italy wasn't important and perhaps I shouldn't have gone, but it was important for Sara to be with her family.

An Indecent Proposal:

While busy searching for the "perfect moment" that Martine McCutcheon had sung about in her 1999 banger 'Perfect Moment' I realised that this heavily choreographed idea I was stressing myself out over was largely formed from proposals I'd scoffed at in films and vomited at on Facebook or Instagram. In my head, it had to be the perfect proposal, but things don't always work out like that, and it's the reasoning and feeling that's the most important thing. It doesn't need to rely on setting or the ideal build-up to be romantic, it's the delivery that counts. Maybe I was just feeling a bit more relaxed about it all now because England were no longer in the World Cup. Sara and I have always shared the opinion that grand gestures are all a bit flashy and unnecessary. Whilst I'd have loved nothing more to propose to the woman of my dreams on the walls of Lucca at dusk (her favourite time of the day), or under the stars in Italy during Nick Cave's performance of 'Into My Arms' there was still a very real possibility I'd have completely ballsed it up. Much like playing the triangle at primary school I could have got my timing wrong and got down on one knee during 'Stagger Lee' as Cave delivered the unequivocal line about sucking someone off at gunpoint or crawling over er...something to get to eh...something else.

I've always found the idea of a public engagement slightly unfair on the person on the receiving end of the proposal. In my mind, public engagements give you an unfair safety net because the likelihood of rejection and your partner lashing out is halved. Take *Gladiators,* for example. People proposed on that show all the time. It got to the point where I started questioning their motives and whether they only went on the show to get battered about by The Wolf enough so they could finally pluck up the courage to ask for their partner's hand in marriage. They'd run up to their already high on emotions partner with their giant foam fingers in the air, pull out a sweaty ring from their sock and pop the question live on television. In doing so, backing them into a corner of the National Indoor Arena in Birmingham they probably weren't thrilled to be in. Even if the contenders didn't win that wouldn't stop them! 'I might not have won tonight Debbie, but because of you I feel like I've won at life.' Of course they all said yes, but I seem to remember one of my sisters once planted the seeds of doubt in my mind when she boldly proclaimed 'You know what, I think she only said yes because there was a camera pointing at her. She'll probably revoke it after the show.'

I went against my instinct, my Facebook wall, the Hollywood scriptwriters and against signing up for a remake of *Gladiators.* Instead, I decided that rather than relying on props, gimmicks, or a crowd of strangers, I'd do it when the moment felt right. And away from any drains to avoid a repeat performance of the infamous Spice Girls necklace incident.

It was early August and Sara was frantically darting back and forth cleaning the flat ahead of her friend arriving from Dublin the next day. I was trying to keep our friends' (Katie & Jeff- who had moved from Sydney to Edinburgh at this point!) small dog Rex entertained and out of mischief as we were pet-sitting him for a couple of days. This is something any dog owner will tell you is an incredibly fine art, and one I was unsurprisingly failing miserably at.

Rex. Gone but not forgotten <3.

I lost sight of Rex for a split second and clocked him again a few moments later. He was sauntering out of the bedroom looking both relieved and guilty which is an immediate red flag that a dog's done something they'd rather you remained blissfully unaware of. I swiftly marched through to the bedroom, past the guilty party and began hunting for clues. Whilst there were no immediate signs of a misdemeanour, given the fact the dog had spun around and was now watching me anxiously from the door with intermittent eye contact, there was definitely something afoot.

After an almost inconclusive search, I spotted my guitar bag poking out from under the bed with a few stray dog hairs (just to be clear, the dog's hairs were stray, I'm not suggesting that my eyes had deduced that they belonged to a stray dog) on it. Sliding out the guitar bag from under the bed, it was drenched and had clearly been the dog's private en-suite for days while he stayed with us.

Rex was an old dog by this point, but that didn't really soften the blow of finding an infinity pool of piss under your bed. Alerting Sara to Rex's toilet habits, I got down on one knee, followed by the other, and proceeded to scrub the floor back to its former glory. After a deep-clean, I hung the soaking guitar bag out the window to dry and sat down on the bed and scrolled through my phone.

Calling Sara through I asked her if she had a few minutes to watch a video. She sat alongside me, and I played her the video I'd made with a special guest appearance from Rex who was providing added percussion and backing vocals scratching at the door outside the room and howling at the moon. As previously mentioned, the video charted our moments together over the years from the early days of working together at the cinema through to Australia and moving into our first flat together in Leith. By this point my heart was beating rapidly like the time I'd smashed a few double vodka Red Bulls in quick succession on a night out with my sisters and thought it was going to leap out of my chest. The song began to fade out as the video cut towards me walking towards our bookcase where I pulled out a leather-bound book with my initials on it which my mum and dad had bought me in Rome when we all went out there to celebrate my dad's 60th the year before. I opened it at the last page and the final words of the book were 'Sara, will you marry me?'

EPILOGUE

There's been a few moments in my life that I look back on and cringe, i.e. throwing a shell in a stranger's swimming pool, inadvertently throwing up on Gemma in the caravan in Germany, not affording my mum more notice about the African shoebox appeal, ghosting my French exam, dying my hair black (twice), dropping out of university in the fashion that I did, taking liberty with the pick and mix in the cinema and knee sliding on a stone floor during karaoke. I look back on them tinged with regret and guilt, perhaps wishing in a way that things had been different whilst also acknowledging the butterfly effect whereby without those incidents, it's highly probable things wouldn't be as they are today.

Setbacks are a necessary requirement to even the scales and make us appreciate the magic moments so they feel all the more special. When I look back at other moments i.e. each Christmas in the Cobb house, watching *Neighbours* with my mum, playing football in the park with my dad, having three great dogs growing up, the 1998/2006/2012 Scottish Cup finals, a family holiday to Turkey in 2004 for my grandpa Paterson's 70th, seeing Oasis in concert, studying Music Business, playing bass for Quiet as a Mouse, moving to Sydney, visiting Hobbiton, the family going to Rome for my dad's 60th in 2017 and Sara saying yes when I asked her to marry me whilst my socks were covered in dog piss, there's not a single thing that could have improved those experiences. (OK, maybe I could have changed my socks.) They were all perfect and a snapshot of just how lucky I am to have lived through those experiences.

Writing a book over the last four years about the people I've met in my life has been an unforgettable experience, and each memory has brought back a host of others that have made this project viable and brought it to life. It's been difficult and deeply moving at times casting my mind back to lost pets and loved ones that I'd compartmentalised in a box at the back of my mind. To have these suddenly slung back to the forefront, often when I least expected it has subsequently heightened my sensitivity and emotional attachment to the stories. It's been equally important for me to leave these bits in as I remember them, and it's been a unique opportunity for me to work through some things, particularly loss of relatives that I now realise I maybe hadn't fully come to terms with prior to jotting them down.

With the books crammed full of amazing memories that I'll forever cherish, I feel I'm now in a place where

I can look forward and focus on making new memories rather than focusing too heavily on what's gone before.

By taking a bit of time to scribble down a few stories, without wanting to sound too arrogant (he writes at the end of a two-part autobiography...) I'd like to think I've forever (or until Amazon go bust) kept these stories and the people in them alive. I hope it's managed to bring back some happy and at times mortifying memories from your own journey through life too. As for whether or not this is the last book, I'll just leave it open-ended and keep you posted if anything else decent happens, i.e. Sara and I's wedding next year or when we become pug parents to Larry and his younger brother Hapax Legomenon.

ACKNOWLEDGE-MENTS

Thank you so much to mum, dad, Sara, Julie, Gemma, Bailey, my grandmas, the rest of my family, John, Kirsty, the Edinburgh/Borders crew, Katie & Jeff, Sandy & Pete and the rest of the Aussie crew, Alex and Quiet as a Mouse, Sara's family, my old flatmates, Rex for being a cracking wingman, John and Nik at Ripping, Mike and Paul at Jewel and Esk, Coutts, Karl at the cinema, Angus Marich, Alan Swan and others for letting me use your amazing photos, Little Indie Blogs and anyone else that's taken time to read any of these books or been part of the stories.

ABOUT THE AUTHOR

Richard Cobb

Richard currently resides in London with his fiancée Sara. He enjoys running, eating biscuits, buying books and not reading them and ruthlessly crushing opponents at Pro Evo.

He has written three other books. The first one sold admirably. The other two probably cost someone in Amazon their job.

He doesn't know why he continues to write this bit in third person when it's blatantly himself that's written it all.

BOOKS BY THIS AUTHOR

Richard Cobb: Part One: The Easier To Digest Years

I've always felt that autobiographies were reserved for the ridiculously famous types in this world like The Rock, Bruce Springsteen or one of the immemorable ones from Blue. Writing an autobiography seemed as elusive as getting a blue tick on Twitter. If you're not famous, off you pop- come back when you've been on Love Island. I'm not famous. You've probably never heard of me. If you have, I'm not the romantic pianist or the sarcastic murderer of the same name (Google it.) I haven't really done that much of note the last thirty years. With that in mind, I decided to write an autobiography.

I used to love posting nonsense on social media about burning toast or faking injury at the gym three seconds into a failed treadmill session. Two days and two likes later (one from my grandma) these stories would be forgotten about. Everyone has pointless anecdotes that they wish they would remember outside the one dimensional airbrushed wall of their Facebook page, but it's basically become a disposable tool, with many of these stories disappearing into the abyss.

If I ever have kids, I'd want them to read about the tin of beans incident in West Linton, video shop culture, the time I threw up on my sister, my numerous failed attempts at love and the time I got a bollocking from the Home Economics teacher that looked like Big Bird from Sesame Street.

I'd also like others to share my pain of having to wear tracksuits, partake in country dancing at school and listen to Steps as a youngster growing up in the '90s.

An Advent Story: (& Other Nonsense Loosely Themed Festive Page Fillers Which Unarguably Didn't Merit A Stand-Alone Book.)

Richard Stewart Haig Cobb, author of the cult hit autobiography 'Richard Cobb: Part One: The easier to digest years' invites you to gather round the piano, sip a warm beverage and listen (by listen, he means read- he hasn't plucked up the courage to ask Neil Oliver to do the audiobook yet, so until then you'll just have to read it in his magnificent long-haired tones) to the story of how he became both fascinated and unreasonably annoyed by Advent calendars and the magic they bring to the most wonderful time of the year.

He also fondly recalls tales of Christmas past, from family sledging adventures on the snowy hills of West Linton, to the sticky dance floors of the infamous Peebles Rugby Club.

There's also a disturbing amount of Macaulay Culkin references for reasons which the author can attest are still very much unclear. A must for fans of his previous work and a 'might as well, it's only 100 pages long and there's pictures' for others.

A Book In A Day

The year is 2020 and we're all invisibly handcuffed to our mobile phones. Social media, fake news and life-affirming videos of people eating spaghetti with scissors battle it out for supremacy and a brief stay in the hotel of our ever eroding attention spans.

One fateful evening after a rather eye-opening glance at my phone's shameful screen time from that day, I decided I really ought to do better and make more of an effort to use my precious time on this planet more wisely.

So I turned the sand timer on its head, put my phone on house arrest in the drawer and set myself an almighty challenge of writing yesterday's wrongs and turning over a short (very short, please don't call it a pamphlet) book in just one day.

What did I write about? Anything and everything that crossed my mind that day that could help people and hopefully make a difference. From the pitfalls of a spoon-fed social media generation, overcoming fears, talking to people more and the feeling that we could all just try a little harder and start being a little more pleasant to one another.